The West German Party System:
An Ecological Analysis
of Social Structure
and Voting Behavior, 1961-1969

DAVID P. CONRADT

University of Florida

 SAGE PUBLICATIONS / Beverly Hills / London

For information address:

SAGE PUBLICATIONS, INC.  SAGE PUBLICATIONS LTD
275 South Beverly Drive   St George's House / 44 Hatton Garden
Beverly Hills, California 90212   London E C 1

International Standard Book Number 0-8039-0146-1

Library of Congress Catalog Card No. 72-77770

FIRST PRINTING

CONTENTS

LIST OF TABLES

The West German Party System:
An Ecological Analysis
of Social Structure
and Voting Behavior, 1961-1969

DAVID P. CONRADT
University of Florida

The 1969 West German election promises to be one of the most intensively studied political events in the short history of the Federal Republic. Social scientists of various theoretical and methodological persuasions have already produced a sizable body of literature on the election and all seem to agree that the 1969 poll, if not a "critical" election in the sense that V. O. Key (1955) developed the concept, still marked an important stage in the development of the Bonn democracy.[1] Students of the party system have focused both on the success of the Social Democrats (SPD) in achieving relative electoral parity with the Christian Democratic Union (CDU) after years of being a distinctly second "major" party, and the continued decline of third and minor parties in spite of an essentially proportional electoral system (Kaltefleiter et al., 1970). At the systemic level, the "turnover" of the major parties in which the Christian Democrats relinquished executive power to the Brandt government after 20 years of rule was regarded by some as a "major

AUTHOR'S NOTE: *The author wishes to express his appreciation to the Foreign Area Fellowship Program for support that enabled him to conduct the initial phases of this research. Data processing and computation facilities were provided by the University of Florida Computing Center. Mrs. Linda Dolive was also of great assistance in preparing the data file. Professors Lewis J. Edinger, Ted Robert Gurr, and Sidney G. Tarrow made numerous helpful comments on an earlier version of this paper.*

innovative breakthrough toward the institutionalization of the post totalitarian regime of 1949" (Edinger, 1970: 550). The inability of antisystem parties, especially the National Democrats (NPD), to gain Bundestag representation and the end of the Grand Coalition, which some observers regarded as congenial to German political cultural values yet detrimental to the institutionalization of liberal democracy, have also been subjects for discussion and analysis (Lehmbruch, 1968; also Kaltefleiter et al., 1970). Finally, the foreign policy output of the new Socialist-Liberal government has focused attention on the international-political consequences of the election and coalition negotiations (Czempiel, 1970; von Beyme, 1970).

This study of recent German electoral behavior attempts to accomplish simultaneous substantive and methodological purposes. Substantively this paper focuses on the interrelationship of social structure, voting behavior, and the West German party system in the 1961-1969 period. Specifically we will seek to explain changes in the character and structure of the party system, which to a great extent became manifest at the 1969 election, by reference to social-structural and behavioral factors. Methodologically the study is designed to examine the potential utility of West German aggregate demographic and electoral data for comparative political analysis. The extent and quality of aggregate data in West Germany have generally been rated quite highly (Hartenstein and Liepelt, 1970).[2] Yet surprisingly few systematic attempts have been made to use these materials in other than a traditional, descriptive manner.[3] In this study we have analyzed these data with a variety of bi- and multivariate statistical techniques in part to ascertain their utility for future historical and cross-national work. Where possible we will also seek to make comparisons between our aggregate findings and those reported by sample survey analysts.

I. THE PROBLEM

At the conclusion of their pioneering theoretical treatise on European party systems Lipset and Rokkan (1968: 50) observed that *"the party systems of the 1960's reflect, with few but significant exceptions, the cleavage structure of the 1920's"* (italics in the original). The West German party system is, of course, one of those "significant exceptions." The unstable, multiparty pattern of the 1920s replete with immobilism and finally in 1933 a disastrous "Caesaristic breakthrough" has not reemerged in the postwar period. What did emerge by 1953, however, was what La Palombara and Weiner (1965: 35) have termed a "hegemonic" party system—i.e., "one in which over an extended period of time the same party, or coalitions dominated by the same party, hold governmental power." The dominant party, the Christian Democratic Union, was also a distinctly postwar creation. At the second Federal election in 1953 the Union increased its percentage of the vote from 31.0% to 45.2% and clearly became the dominant party in the developing postwar party system. This was West Germany's "critical" postwar election.[4] Interest was high, the major parties were clearly polarized on domestic and foreign policies, and significant shifts took place in the sociological composition of the parties' vote. Specifically, the Union absorbed a large share of the third and splinter party vote, e.g., the German Party (DP), the Bavarian Party (BP) and various other regional and special interest parties. In 1957, the Christian Democrats, still led by Adenauer, secured an absolute majority of seats. Although the party needed a coalition partner after the elections of 1961 and 1965, its choice, the Free Democrats (FDP) was a distinctly junior partner. The point is clear: no national government without the dominant participation of the Christian Democrats was possible from 1953-1965.

The *Machtwechsel* of October 1969, i.e., the alternation of the major parties for the first time, may indicate that the West German party system is in transition from a stable "hegemonic" system to a stable turnover system, i.e., one in which "there is relatively frequent change in the party that governs or in the party that dominates a coalition" (La Palombara and Weiner, 1965: 35). Regardless of how the present system is classified, the CDU for the first time in its history finds itself in opposition. What factors—social-structural and political—can explain these changes and what are their implications for the future of the party system? This is the substantive question that will concern us here.

II. THE GRAND COALITION AND STRATEGIC ALTERNATIVES

Before proceeding to the analysis of the aggregate demographic and electoral data, a short summary of the major strategic alternatives confronting the three Bundestag parties prior to and during the campaign is in order. Of particular importance, of course, is the effect of the three-year Grand Coalition between the CDU/CSU and the SPD upon their conception of the campaign and election.

A. THE CHRISTIAN DEMOCRATS

In five previous campaigns the central focus of the Union's electoral appeal had been on its Chancellor. This stress on the Chancellor was functional for both party unity and electoral success. The rise of the CDU paralleled the personal successes of Adenauer and Erhard. As a loose alliance of extremely diverse interests, intraparty consensus on policy was difficult, if not impossible to achieve. In the absence of any real programmatic unity, the CDU has simply emphasized in vague, general terms that it has the *Fuehrung,* the leadership, necessary to govern Germany. In this context concern with programmatic development was, given the personal successes of Adenauer and Erhard, electorally superfluous and from the standpoint of party unity, potentially divisive.

More than any other party the Christian Democrats were also able to cloak themselves with the mantle of state authority, an important advantage in the statist German political culture. In addition, the Union's previous appeals also relied heavily on West Germany's postwar economic prosperity, which it attempted to credit solely to itself. The "Chancellor effect" together with economic prosperity were both projected in a general security theme, that was common to all CDU campaigns: the CDU Chancellor had and would continue to maintain Germany's national security through her alliance with the United States as well as ensuring general domestic prosperity, peace, and tranquility. It had been a winning formula.

In 1969, however, this traditional approach was complicated by three new factors. First the Union had to share the political-governmental stage for the first time with the Social Democrats. In previous elections the party had no major coalition partner to share the credit with (and place the blame on, if possible); it had only to contend with the sometimes rebellious but always small Free Democrats (1949, 1953, 1961, 1965) and/or minor splinter parties (1949, 1953, 1957). But in 1969 the party could hardly deny that it had shared governmental responsibility with the Social Democrats or that the SPD had made substantial contributions to the Grand Coalition. Thus the Union had to campaign on the record of the coalition as a whole and not on its record as the sole governing party, or as the clearly dominant party in a *Kleine Koalition.*

A second complicating factor was the presence and undisputed electoral appeal of the SPD's Economics Minister, Karl Schiller, and the absence of a comparable figure the Union could call its own. In previous campaigns the Christian Democrats could not only claim the Chancellorship and overall responsibility for the *Richtlinien der Politik,* but it could also project itself as the party that gave Germans economic security and prosperity. The main vehicle for this latter claim was, of course, Ludwig Erhard. But by 1969 Erhard was largely forgotten; according to one study only 41% of a national sample of electors could remember that he was the Union's *Kanzlerkandidat* in 1965 (Kaase, 1970: 68). The Union had clearly lost its ascendancy in this area to Schiller and the SPD.

Finally the Union's strategic plans were complicated by a new competitor on the right, the National Democrats. The NPD had by virtue of its successes in state elections, its fairly well-articulated organizational structure, and adequate (a 10 million DM budget for the 1969 election) finances, become a major alternative for that segment of the electorate (estimated at 10-12%) who were attracted to the party's strong conservative, antisystem appeal. CDU leaders were concerned that the NPD would "pass the Union on the right" to the point where the party could secure Bundestag representation sufficient to deny the CDU/CSU an absolute majority of seats or reduce its plurality over the Social Democrats. Public opinion polls had shown that the NPD had impressive potential support among farmers and independent nonmanuals in rural areas as well as among refugees and traditional national-conservatives (Klingemann and Pappi, 1968: 9ff). In past elections, especially those of 1961 and 1965, the Union had secured high majorities among these groups, but in 1969 support from these segments of the electorate could not be taken for granted.

This concern over the possible loss of conservative, nationalist voters to the NPD is one explanation for the more nationalist stance adopted by Chancellor Kiesinger in the spring of 1969. The Chancellor's refusal to reevaluate the Deutsche Mark (DM), or to sign the nuclear nonproliferation treaty, together with his strong defense of the Hallstein doctrine following Cambodia's recognition of the DDR, were seen as part of a campaign to limit CDU/CSU defections to the National Democrats by adding a "touch of nationalism" to the Union's campaign.

But in spite of this complicated strategic situation, the Union still had several advantages over its rivals. First, the popularity of Chancellor Kiesinger remained high and indeed increased as the campaign progressed. The Chancellor ran well ahead of Brandt, and toward the end of the campaign he was also well ahead of his own party (see Tables 1 and 2). Not surprisingly the CDU/CSU essentially presented itself to the electorate through the image of Kiesinger—*auf den Kanzler kommt es an* (it is the Chancellor who counts)—was a prominent slogan. The party's election posters all featured Kiesinger and stressed the importance of leadership— "Coalitions come and go, but leadership must remain." This leadership

TABLE 1
Chancellor Preference March-September 1969 (in percentages)

Date	Kiesinger	Brandt	Neither of the Two	Strauss	Schiller	Don't Know/ No Answer
March 1969	39	13	—	10	5	33
May 1969	43	19	—	12	4	22
July 1969	42	19	—	10	5	24
August 1969	60	24	13	—	—	3
September 1969	52	28	16	—	—	4

SOURCE: Institut fuer Sozialwissenschaften der Universitaet Mannheim, "Daten zur Bundestagswahl 1969," Mannheim, January 1970: 39. The relevant question texts were, from March to July: "After the next Bundestag election, the parties must once again select a Head of Government, a Federal Chancellor. Whom would you prefer most as Federal Chancellor?" In the August and September surveys the question was: "Now I would like very much to know who you would prefer most as Federal Chancellor: Kurt-Georg Kiesinger or Willy Brandt?" The absence of Strauss and Schiller in the August and September surveys was apparently due to the different formulation of the question.

theme was then closely connected with the traditional projection of the Union as the guardian of socioeconomic, political, and military security. [5]

In line with this stress on the continuity and stability of CDU leadership, the events of late 1966 and the SPD's role in the Grand Coalition were deemphasized. The Social Democrats were regarded as just one of many coalition partners the Union had had since 1949; it too was just a junior partner.

Secondly, Union also hoped to offset possible losses to the SPD and NPD through gains from former FDP voters discontented with their party's move to the left. CDU/CSU leaders attempted to label the new

TABLE 2
Party Preference March-September 1969

Date	CDU/CSU	SPD	FDP	NPD	Other	Don't Know/ No Answer
March 1969	38	46	6	2	1	7
May 1969	43	41	5	2	1	8
July 1969	44	42	5	2	1	6
August 1969	52	39	3	1	1	4
September 1969	44	42	5	1	1	7

SOURCE: See Table 1. The sample sizes were March 1969: 1573; May 1969: 1587; July 1969: 1451; August 1969: 958; September 1969: 915.

FDP leadership as unreliable and irresponsible especially in the foreign policy issue area (Der Spiegel, 1969a: 28). The FDP was pictured as a party which had lost its way and was now dangerously close to forsaking the principles and policies which had made it an acceptable partner of the Union in five cabinets.

There is some evidence that this hope of gaining votes from defecting Free Democrats was well founded. In previous campaigns, voting studies (Klingemann and Pappi, 1970) had revealed a mutual interchange between CDU/CSU and FDP supporters. This was especially prevalent, of course, during the 1961 and 1965 campaigns. Since the March 1969 Heinemann election, however, polls had shown that this exchange now yielded a net benefit for the Union. According to Klingemann and Pappi (1970) the Free Democrats by the spring of 1969 were securing almost all of their new supporters from the ranks of former SPD voters and previous nonvoters.

Thirdly, a wave of wildcat strikes in early September appeared to halt the extensive migration of middle-class voters to the Social Democrats. The Union attempted to link the SPD with this industrial unrest and pointed to the strikes as an example of the instability and recklessness that would accompany an SPD government pursuing irresponsible economic policies.[6]

1. Coalition Plans

The Union's most preferred outcome would have been, of course, an absolute majority, yet the party's leadership regarded this as extremely unlikely (Zundel, 1969d: 3). The Union's second choice was a renewal of the Grand Coalition with it as the dominant party, i.e., still holding the Chancellorship. In the event of a renewal of the Grand Coalition, the Union's leadership hoped that a new Anglo-American type of electoral system would be quickly passed.

A "small" coalition with the FDP was only the third preference of the CDU. The party's leadership, however, was extremely skeptical about the willingness of the FDP to reestablish the old middle-class alignment, even if the election outcome made such a coalition mathematically possible. Changes in the FDP since 1966 had been designed to remove the image of a CDU satellite that the party had acquired during the 1949-1956 and 1961-1966 coalitions.

The fourth possibility—opposition—was one dreaded by most party leaders, although there is some indication that the younger reform-minded elements in the party would and did welcome this outcome.

During the 1969 campaign itself this strategic design proved unwork-able in one important area: the plan for a personalized contest between Kiesinger and Brandt. Instead much of the party and Chancellor's campaign efforts were directed not at Brandt, but at Karl Schiller. The vehicle for this conflict was the D-Mark reevaluation issue, by far the most important one during the campaign. Since early 1968 Karl Schiller, SPD Economics Minister in the Kiesinger cabinet, had advocated an upward reevaluation of the Mark in order to avoid a general inflation, which he contended would result from Germany's continuing high export surpluses. The Christian Democrats and especially Chancellor Kiesinger and Finance Minister Strauss opposed a reevaluation. At the time of the November 1968 monetary crisis Kiesinger publicly pledged that he would never reevaluate the Mark as long as he was Chancellor (Frankfurter Allegemeine Zeitung, 1968). The Union argued that the best check against inflation would be a reduction in governmental spending, increased taxation, and higher tax credits to importers. Reform of the international monetary system was, according to the CDU/CSU, the primary responsibility of countries with "sick" currencies, not nations whose currencies were "strong and healthy" (Der Spiegel, 1969c).

This issue of Mark reevaluation became electorally significant because it could be linked to "prices" and "inflation," two central concerns of German voters.[7] The memories of the disastrous 1923 inflation and the monetary instability of the immediate postwar years were still present among large segments of the electorate (Institut fuer Demoskopie, 1968: 268ff). In tapping this concern for economic stability and prosperity the CDU/CSU in previous elections had enjoyed a considerable advantage over the Social Democrats. In past campaigns the party could convincingly claim that it deserved major credit for Germany's economic prosperity. But in 1969 the CDU had no *Wirtschaftskopf* to match Schiller in voter appeal (Simon, 1969: 22). As Economics Minister, Schiller was given most of the credit for ending the 1966-1967 recession and returning the German economy to its "boom" condition.[8] Moreover in the reevaluation issue Schiller was credited by mass publics with having better judgment as to what Germany's policy should be than either Strauss or Kiesinger.[9]

According to some reports (Zundel, 1969c: 1) it was Schiller's relentless advocacy of upward reevaluation and the impact of this issue on public opinion which led to the "heating up" of the campaign in the late spring of 1969. The Social Democrats and Schiller attempted to label Kiesinger and Strauss as economic innocents, whose stubborn refusal to reevaluate would mean higher prices and runaway inflation. Thus the center-right Christian Democrats were put in the unique and uncomfortable position of having to defend themselves against Socialist charges that they were incompetent to make policy for Germany's "free market economy."

B. THE SOCIAL DEMOCRATS

In the two previous post-Bad Godesberg campaigns the SPD had sought to deemphasize its differences with the Christian Democrats. The campaigns of 1961 and 1965 were strongly influenced by the Wehner strategy of "embracing the middle," which called for a programmatic shift into the center of the West German political spectrum with a resultant deemphasis of the party's traditional working-class image and its policies regarding nationalization of industry, economic planning, church-state relations, and foreign and defense policies. [10] These campaigns focused instead on the party's leader, Willy Brandt, and were characterized by an extensive employment of modern advertising and public relations techniques designed to "sell" the "new" Social Democrats to especially the traditionally conservative, middle-class segments of the West German electorate.

But in contrast to 1961 and 1965 the Social Democrats in 1969 did not attempt to focus their appeal on Brandt. The two previous campaigns and numerous polls over a ten-year period had clearly shown that Brandt as a personality did not have a broad affective base in the electorate sufficient to bring the SPD a Bundestag majority. [11] This was also true of the 1969 campaign; as Table 1 shows, Kiesinger was consistently favored over Brandt throughout 1969. In a personalized campaign against Kiesinger, it was reasoned, Brandt would have been the loser just as he was in 1961 and 1965 when pitted against Adenauer and Erhard. Over this period Brandt has continuously run behind the SPD while the CDU Chancellor has secured more support than his party. This difference may be due, of course, to the office of Chancellor itself; the present Brandt Chancellorship offers the first opportunity to test this hypothesis of a "Chancellor effect" or statist-bonus to the holder of the office (Kaase, 1970: 71-72; Eberlein, 1968: 37). [12]

Given this fact of political life, the SPD concentrated on projecting the collective accomplishments of its ministers in the Grand Coalition and linking their efforts to a general modernization theme (Zundel, 1969d: 3).

But as in the case of the CDU/CSU, the campaign strategy of the SPD was also complicated by the party's participation in the Grand Coalition. The Social Democrats were faced with the dilemma that the increase in support for its policies and leaders (especially Schiller and Brandt) was closely related to general approval of the Grand Coalition as a whole. That is, those segments of the electorate which became favorably oriented toward the SPD as a result of the party's successful participation in the Kiesinger cabinet, were also strong supporters of the Grand Coalition arrangement. The SPD strategists were thus confronted with the problem of projecting the party's accomplishments in the Grand Coalition without thereby endangering the coalition itself.

The stress on the party's substantive performance in the Kiesinger cabinet was also regarded as a solution to this dilemma. The Social Democrats also largely restricted their criticism of the Union to the CDU's policies prior to and during the 1966-1967 recession; no direct attacks were made until the end of the campaign on Kiesinger or the CDU ministers for their performance after the SPD became their partner. However, it was suggested that the Christian Democrats, without the SPD, were unable to guarantee economic growth and job security. Thus the Social Democrats attempted to revive the electorate's memory of the confusion and uncertainty that characterized the West-German political scene after the collapse of the Erhard government. And indeed, largely through Schiller's efforts, for the first time in German history, economic prosperity and the Social Democrats were closely associated by large segments of the electorate. For example, almost 40% of a 1969 sample agreed with the statement: "We have Schiller to thank that we're all doing well again." Schiller's score on this question was almost 10% higher than Ludwig Erhard's in 1965. Between 1965 and 1969 the percentage of respondents in national surveys attributing greater competence in economic matters to the Christian Democrats dropped from 37 to 31% while the percentage favoring the SPD rose from 25 to 32% (Noelle-Neumann, 1969: 3-4).

The party's strategists thus hoped to make sizable inroads into the middle-class vote by virtue of its entrance into and successful performance in the Grand Coalition. Also for the first time in over a generation the Social Democrats, through their participation in the government, had a legitimate and convincing claim to the mantle of state authority—an important asset in the German political culture where state authority, embodied by corps of expert, objective *Beamten* remains superior to mere civil society with its conflicts and competition between parties and interest groups (Dahrendorf, 1967), while in opposition, the SPD had been at a disadvantage in being unable to project itself as a *Staatspartei*. But in 1969 the party had become a beneficiary of this cultural trait, which continues to be regarded by many as an impediment to democratic stability in Germany.

1. Coalition Plans

The SPD's first preference would have been to govern alone. However, few if any of the party's leaders expected an absolute majority; this was publicly acknowledged at numerous times throughout the campaign (Frankfurter Allgemeine Zeitung, 1969).

In contrast to the CDU/CSU the SPD's second preference was a coalition with the Free Democrats. By the late spring of 1969 it became apparent that the party was aiming for this "small coalition" instead of contenting itself with a renewal of the Grand Coalition. This latter alternative was generally ranked third by most party leaders.

The decision to aim for a coalition with the FDP was not reached, however, without considerable discussion and disagreement within the party leadership. One faction, centering around Helmut Schmidt and Conrad Ahlers, preferred a renewal of the coalition together with an electoral law change.[13] These *Etatists* considered the overall success of the Grand Coalition more important than the SPD's record within it. They argued that the FDP was still unreliable and too wedded to big business in its economic and social welfare policies to be an acceptable partner. Furthermore this group doubted whether the SPD and FDP could achieve an absolute majority of seats especially if the NPD were to secure Bundestag representation (Der Spiegel 28, 1969a: 26-27).[14] This pro-Grand Coalition faction would also have preferred a "quiet" campaign in 1969 on the Austrian model. While this faction still regarded the Grand Coalition as only an intermediate stage on the SPD's road to becoming Germany's "natural" governing party, they contended that a further period of alignment with the Union was needed.

But a second faction within the leadership led by Brandt, Heinemann, and SPD *Land* leaders from Hesse, Schleswig-Holstein, and Nordrhein-Westfalen wanted above all a coalition with the Free Democrats. This group was later joined by Wehner and became dominant. While most of this faction had participated in the Grand Coalition, they had been careful to emphasize SPD accomplishments and to maintain a critical detachment to the Union and Chancellor Kiesinger (Zundel: 1969d). The Brandt wing contended that the FDP had changed and that the bulk of its electorate and leadership wanted a coalition with the SPD. In addition the virtual unanimity of the foreign and defense policies of the two parties as well as the realistic prospect that 20 years of CDU rule could be ended were also stressed. They urged, therefore, that a hard confrontative campaign be fought against the Union with the chief goal being a *Machtwechsel* via a coalition with the Free Democrats.

C. THE FREE DEMOCRATS

For the Free Democrats the election was the most critical in the party's history. As a third party with no chance of forming a government alone and always in danger of falling below the 5% level, the party had to structure its campaign so as to maximize its bargaining potential in the postelection coalition negotiations. Its chief goal was to win sufficient mandates to prevent either a renewal of the Grand Coalition or an absolute CDU/CSU majority.[15] Either of these two latter outcomes would have meant the passage of a new "first-past-the-post" electoral law. Such an electoral system would probably eliminate the party as a significant political force. Since 1957 it has won no district contests and has been totally dependent on the proportional distribution of mandates from the party lists for its Bundestag representation.

Thus the FDP sought once again to become the needed "pivot party" in the Bundestag. Of the two possible coalition partners, the party's leadership and most, but by no means all, of its voters preferred the Social Democrats.[16] A remake of the old "middle-class" coalition with the CDU/CSU would have badly split the party. Both the younger FDP members and the new supporters it had acquired since the Grand Coalition had little sympathy for the CDU/CSU.[17] Yet even a coalition with the CDU/CSU would probably have been preferred to opposition and eventual extinction through a new electoral law.

Since the Grand Coalition, the FDP had sought through a series of policy and leadership changes to demonstrate that it was not a mere satellite of the CDU/CSU. It was hoped that with a slight move to the left the party would become more attractive to both CDU/CSU and SPD supporters discontented with the Grand Coalition and at the same time convince the Social Democrats that it could be an acceptable and reliable coalition partner (Strobel, 1968: 5). In September 1967, the party's National Chairman during the 1961-1966 coalition with the CDU/CSU, Erich Mende, resigned and was succeeded by Walter Scheel. Scheel was generally regarded as a "progressive" Liberal who wanted to make the party "open on all sides." Together with other progressive FDP leaders such as Wilhelm Moersch, Hildegard Hamm-Bruecher, and Hans Wilhelm Genscher, Scheel attempted, in spite of the small size of the FDP *Fraktion*, to mount a vigorous opposition in the Bundestag. In domestic politics, the party strongly opposed the Emergency Laws *(Notstandsgesetze)* and put forth far-reaching proposals for education, legal, and tax reform. In contrast to most CDU/CSU deputies, it also supported the liberal neo-Keynesian economic policies of Karl Schiller. In foreign policy questions, where the party had diverged considerably from the CDU/CSU even during the Adenauer era, the FDP advocated a more "mobile" approach to the problems of reunification and *Ostpolitik* that even went beyond SPD proposals. A treaty with East Germany was proposed together with a unilateral renouncement of nuclear weapons and Germany's unconditional assent to the nuclear nonproliferation treaty.

The clearest demonstration, however, of the party's intent to change its course was the support it gave to the SPD's candidate at the election of the Federal President in March 1969. The election of the SPD candidate (Gustav Heinemann) with near-unanimous FDP support set off a wave of speculation about the possibility of a Socialist-Liberal coalition after the September balloting. There is also some evidence that the action of the FDP delegates initiated a wave of defections on the part of conservative FDP voters to the Union. But on balance the Free Democrats' *aperatura a sinistra* appeared to be meeting with moderate electoral success. In the last two state elections prior to the Federal election (Bremen, October 1967, and Baden-Wuerttemberg, April 1968) the FDP, in view of the competition for the anti-Grand Coalition vote provided by the NPD, made encouraging gains.

The social bases of the party's electorate were also changing. Between 1966 and 1968 the FDP became less a preserve of the Protestant middle-class and somewhat more of a broadly based *Volkspartei*. Among Protestant manual workers, for example, the party by 1968 had achieved support roughly proportionate to this group's representation in the total electorate (Zundel, 1969a). The FDP had made some gains among those social groups which traditionally had regarded it as the "party of the upper ten-thousand."[18]

These leadership, policy, and clientele changes represented a considerable self-transformation for the party. Their purpose was in part to exploit what some observers regarded as a growing discontent with the Grand Coalition among sizable sections of the electorate. Opinion surveys (Zentralarchiv Data Pool, 1969) had shown that from 25 to 30% of German voters had an essentially negative orientation toward the Grand Coalition and, furthermore, that roughly one-fourth of this group regarded voting for the FDP as the best means of expressing this dissatisfaction with the major parties and their coalition.[19] The party's strategists thus calculated that if the FDP could retain its hard-core electorate and add those voters discontented with the Grand Coalition, it could secure 12 to 15% of the party vote. But this strategy depended upon the party's ability to avoid driving its hard-core electorate into the ranks of the CDU/CSU by moving too far to the left as well as the maintenance of stable relations between the major parties, i.e., the continuation of the Grand Coalition. If the SPD-CDU/CSU alignment were to end, or even if the coalition parties polarized during the campaign, this strategy would be in danger. Thus the party had to strike a balance between maintaining its traditional clientele while at the same time being sufficiently progressive to attract the anti-Grand Coalition voter (Zundel, 1969a). This latter progressive direction was also necessary to demonstrate to the Social Democrats that the party would be an acceptable partner.

Unfortunately for the Free Democrats none of these conditions was fulfilled. First, the coalition partners increasingly differentiated themselves from each other to the point where the alignment was de facto at an end. This heating-up or politization of the campaign became apparent by the spring of 1969. The main vehicle for this development was the reevaluation issue and the intensity with which this issue was debated by Schiller and Kiesinger (Zundel, 1969b). This polarization of the coalition parties made it increasingly difficult for the FDP to hold its newly won supporters from the ranks of those discontented with the Grand Coalition. With the differences between the coalition partners accentuated, the rationale for supporting the FDP as a protest against the CDU-SPD alignment became less tenable. This development coincided with an FDP decline in opinion polls (Zentralarchiv Data Pool, 1969).

The FDP leadership also failed to follow through with its original plan of expressing no preference during the campaign for either of the major parties as a coalition partner. Instead the party's leadership late in the campaign left little doubt that the Social Democrats were the preferred partner (Zundel, 1969e). This decision, which represented a departure from the original campaign plan, has been identified as a major factor in the party's loss of much of its traditional electorate. According to some surveys, the FDP lost roughly half of its 1965 middle-class supporters to the CDU and NPD, with most of these defections taking place in the last few weeks of the campaign.[20] It has also been suggested (Weyer, 1970) that had the party centered its campaign strategy around the goal of a Socialist-Liberal government and projected itself as a middle-class corrective to the SPD, it would have made sizable gains among reform-minded segments of the electorate which desired the end of the CDU/CSU rule, but who were still hesitant about supporting the SPD.[21] In short after the de facto end of the Grand Coalition, the party gave its newly won post-1966 supporters no rationale for not supporting the Social Democrats in preference to the FDP.

III. VOTING BEHAVIOR AND THE PARTY SYSTEM

A. THE MAJOR PARTIES

1. Social Democrats

The clear winner of the election was the SPD. With 42.7% of the party vote and 228 seats (127 direct district victories), the Social Democrats achieved their fourth consecutive gain in Bundestag elections. These results appear to have vindicated the party's controversial decision in 1966 to enter into a coalition with the CDU/CSU. Although still Germany's "second" major party, the SPD's performance represented a sharp turnabout from the successive declines the party had experienced in state elections held after the formation of the Grand Coalition. Indeed at the *Landtagswahl* in Baden-Wuerttemberg, the last before the 1969 poll, the Social Democrats dropped below the 30% level for the first time since 1957.[22] And as late as June 1969, most polls still showed the SPD trailing the Christian Democrats by 10-12%. What factors can explain this rise between April 1968 (the Baden-Wuerttemberg election) and the September 1969 Federal Election?

As pointed out above, the SPD leadership hoped that the party's participation in the Grand Coalition and the performance of its key ministers, particularly Schiller and Brandt, would enable it to make inroads into those parts of the electorate traditionally reluctant to support the Social Democrats. Above all the SPD was hoping for gains among Catholic and middle-class voters. The previous inability of the Social Democrats to achieve electoral parity with the CDU/CSU was due essentially to the party's relatively poor performance among these groups of electors (Liepelt and Mitscherlich, 1968). Also numerous voting studies, based upon both survey and aggregate data, have found that social class and religion have been the two major demographic factors structuring the party vote (Linz, 1960; Kaase, 1970). To what extent, then, can SPD gains at the 1969 election be explained by changes in these sections of the electorate?

(a) *The religion factor.* In examining the election results by the religious composition of the districts, we see that during the 1957-1969 period the SPD registered both greater relative and absolute gains in Catholic seats than in Protestant or "Mixed" constituencies (Table 3).[23] For the 1965-1969 period, the SPD change Index in these Catholic seats was 110.6 compared with 109.1 in the Protestant districts and 108.1 in the heterogeneous constituencies.[24] As Table 3 indicates, the Social

TABLE 3
Mean Major Party Vote 1957-1969[a] by Religious
Composition of District

	1957	1961	1965	1969
Catholic (n=85)				
SPD	22.7	27.4	31.4	34.6
CDU/CSU	62.9	58.1	58.1	55.4
FDP	5.6	10.1	7.7	4.8
NPD	—	—	1.6	3.9
Protestant (n=95)				
SPD	35.9	40.7	42.3	46.2
CDU/CSU	40.1	36.2	41.7	41.3
FDP	8.8	15.8	11.6	6.6
NPD	—	—	2.6	4.9
Mixed (n=68)				
SPD	36.3	39.5	43.4	46.8
CDU/CSU	49.9	43.5	44.0	42.3
FDP	8.2	12.2	8.8	5.8
NPD	—	—	1.8	4.0

a. Minor party votes have been omitted.

TABLE 4
Mean Party Vote 1965-1969 by District Type[a] (in percentages)

	SPD		CDU/CSU		FDP		NPD	
District Type	1965	1969	1965	1969	1965	1969	1965	1969
Metropolitan- Catholic	39.4	45.4	47.9	43.1	9.1	6.3	1.9	3.8
Metropolitan- Protestant	46.3	51.4	37.9	36.2	11.1	7.0	2.2	3.9
Metropolitan- Mixed	46.7	50.2	39.4	37.6	9.4	6.6	2.1	4.3
Industrial- Catholic	32.6	36.1	57.3	54.5	7.3	4.8	1.3	3.6
Industrial- Protestant	43.1	46.2	41.4	41.6	11.4	6.3	2.6	4.9
Industrial- Mixed	44.0	47.2	44.6	42.7	8.2	5.3	1.5	3.7
Rural-Catholic	26.8	28.4	63.4	61.8	7.2	4.1	1.7	4.2
Rural-Protestant	37.3	40.4	46.3	46.1	12.5	6.6	2.9	6.0
Rural-Mixed	29.2	32.3	57.6	56.5	10.0	5.7	2.0	4.9

a. Minor party votes have been omitted.

Democrats, while still a distinctly second party in Catholic areas, have nonetheless made steady progress over the last four Bundestag elections. Not surprisingly, as Wildenmann (1969: 15) and his associates have found, this has also been the case for state elections. In all *Landtagswahlen* between 1963 and 1968 the SPD made greater relative gains in Catholic regions than in Protestant areas.

The 1969 result represents then the continuation of a trend discernible in Bundestag elections at least since 1957. [25] In Protestant and "Mixed" seats, the SPD already had a plurality over the CDU by 1965. From the perspective of the religious factor alone, the Christian Democrats retained their national edge over the Social Democrats in 1969 on the strength of their still commanding majority in Catholic districts. Nevertheless, the CDU/CSU losses were still greatest in these regions; the party's mean decline between 1965 and 1969 was 2.7% in these 95 constituencies as opposed to 0.4% in Protestant seats and 1.7% in Mixed constituencies. The correlation between the CDU/CSU and SPD change indices, controlling for the effects of the FDP and NPD vote, was $-.69$ in the Catholic seats, in the Protestant districts this partial r was $-.44$ and in Mixed constituencies only $-.12$. This would also seem to indicate that competition between the major parties was sharper in these Catholic areas than in Protestant or Mixed regions. Also, the mean "swing" to the SPD between 1965 and 1969 was greater in Catholic seats (6.2%) than in Mixed (5.2%) or Protestant (4.8%) districts. [26]

Unfortunately, these aggregate data do not allow us to further explore the various, particularly psychological dimensions of this rise of support for the SPD in Catholic districts. Earlier evidence from survey data, however, has shown a steady increase in support for the SPD especially among Catholics with a "weak" attachment to the church as measured by church attendance and in some studies the respondent's self-estimation of his attachment *(Bindung)* to religion. In one study (Blankenburg, 1967: 47-48) conducted in Nordrhein-Westfalen West Germany's largest *Land,* support for the SPD among Catholics who "seldom" or "never" attended church rose from 50% in 1962 to 64% in 1966 (recall question); among "occasionally" attending Catholics, preference for the SPD increased from 35% to 45% during this period, but among those Catholic voters who regularly attended services, support for the SPD rose only slightly (15% to 17%) over the 1962-1966 time span.

Since, however, most Catholics (60% according to recent polls) are still regular church goers, the total national effect of Socialist gains among "weak" Catholics has been limited. On the other hand, surveys over the past fifteen years have also shown a steady decline in church attendance among both confessions. This may be the key to explaining the steady SPD gains that have taken place. However, this question of whether the 1969 SPD rise in Catholic districts was due primarily to the continued decline of general attachment to the church, or to SPD inroads into the "hard-core" Catholic vote, or to some other factor such as age or upward-mobility is a question that must await the more detailed analysis of survey data.

(b) *Social class factor.* With these aggregate materials, it is not possible, of course, to make definitive statements about the support given by middle-class electors to the SPD from 1961-1969. However, since the occupational composition (based on the 1961 Census) of each electoral district is known, we can make some inferences about the structure of the party vote in demographically diverse seats.

To facilitate this part of our analysis, the 248 election districts were divided into three types—metropolitan-white collar, industrial, and rural—on the basis of the distribution of its work force. *Metropolitan districts* were those in which the percentage of civil servants and salaried nonmanuals *(Angestellte)* exceeded 30% (national mean = 26.0%). These 71 districts were all located in cities with a population above 200,000 (mean number of inhabitants per sq. kilometer: 2,357). The 105 *Industrial districts* were those in which the manual worker segment of the work force exceeded 48% (national mean: 45.6%). These districts were in distinctly less urban areas (mean population density 629.5). Finally the remaining 72 constituencies were easily clasisfied as *Rural;* the percentage of independent nonmanuals and farmers exceeded 25% (national mean: 20.9) and the number of inhabitants per square kilometer was a very low 117.9. This threefold occupational classification produced no overlapping constituencies. A summary of the demographic characteristics of each type is

TABLE 5
Mean Major Party[a] Vote 1961-1969 by Constituency Type

Party	Metropolitan (n=71)			Industrial (n=105)			Rural (n=72)		
	1961	1965	1969	1961	1965	1969	1961	1965	1969
SPD	40.9	44.6	49.4	37.5	40.8	44.1	28.2	30.7	32.9
CDU/ CSU	39.7	41.1	38.6	44.5	46.4	45.2	53.4	56.9	55.8
FDP	14.6	10.0	6.7	12.5	9.3	5.6	11.7	9.3	5.1
NPD	—	2.1	4.0	—	1.9	4.1	—	2.2	4.9

a. Minor party percentages for these years have been omitted.

presented in Appendix B: for further analysis the three district types were sometimes subdivided by their religious composition—Catholic, Protestant, or Mixed—which produced a total of 9 district types: Metropolitan-Catholic (n = 19), -Protestant (n = 26), and -Mixed (n = 26); Industrial-Catholic (n = 26), -Protestant (n = 43), and -Mixed (n = 36); Rural-Catholic (n = 40), -Protestant (n = 25), and -Mixed (n = 7).

We see in Table 5 that SPD gains were largest in the Metropolitan/ White-Collar seats. In those 70 districts with over 30% of the work force in white-collar occupations the SPD vote since 1961 has increased by 8.5% in contrast to 6.6% in the Industrial seats and 4.7% in the Rural constituencies. Over the 1965-1969 period, the mean swing to the SPD in these Metropolitan/White-Collar constituencies was 8.2% as opposed to 4.6% in the Industrial seats and 3.7% in the Rural districts. In the Metropolitan/White-Collar districts, the Social Democrats have steadily widened their margin over the CDU/CSU since 1961. In 1969, even the combined CDU/CSU-FDP percentage, the old Adenauer-Erhard coalition, did not exceed that of the Social Democrats.

In examining the simple correlates of the SPD vote over the 1957-1969 period (Table 6), we see that the correlation between the percentage of white-collar workers in a district and the SPD vote has risen from +.37 in 1957 to +.64 in 1969. As Table 7 shows, the Social Democrats have over the past four national elections become a more middle-class (or at least nonmanual) party.[27] Two indicators of urbanization—population density and the percentage of district inhabitants living in multiple-unit dwellings—have also tended to correlate more highly with the SPD vote over the 1957-1969 period. The manual worker variable, according to these simple correlation coefficients, has remained fairly constant. This would seem to indicate that this particular segment of the electorate has yielded few gains for the SPD in the 1960s and indeed Social Democratic gains in Industrial seats have not been as large as those in Metropolitan/ White-Collar constituencies.

Not surprisingly, the correlation between several key demographic variables and the SPD vote is also higher in the 85 Catholic constituencies. Table 7 presents these coefficients for 1969 broken down by the religious composition of the district. Especially evident is the sharp rise in the SPD/white-collar correlation in the Catholic districts. Even when controlling for the effects of the Protestant variable in these districts, this relationship remains essentially unchanged (partial r = +.83). This would seem to indicate that SPD strength and gains in the Metropolitan-Catholic seats were not restricted to the Protestant areas of these constituencies; the inference is clear: the Social Democrats made inroads into the middle-class Catholic segment of the electorate.

TABLE 6

Main Demographic Correlates of SPD Vote 1957-1969[a]

Variable	1957	1961	1965	1969
Salaried nonmanuals in district	.37	.51	.55	.64
Inhabitants in multiple-unit dwellings	na	.58	.67	.70
Population density	.45	.47	.57	.61
Protestants in district	.55	.63	.52	.53
Manual workers in district	.28	.41	.45	.41
Farmers in district	−.71	−.67	−.74	−.78

a. Entries are Pearsonian correlation coefficients computed on the basis of percentages. The 1957 percentages for the demographic variables are taken from the 1950 Census; those for 1961-1969 are from the 1961 Census. The party vote percentages are those from the second (party list) part of the ballot. The unit of analysis is the Bundestag election district (1957: n=247; 1961-1969: n=248).

TABLE 7

Some Correlates of the 1969 SPD Vote by the Religious Composition of the District (in percentages)

	Catholic (n=85)	Protestant (n=95)	Mixed (n=68)	Nationwide (n=248)
Variable	r	r	r	r
White-collar workers and civil servants	.85	.59	.49	.64
Manual workers	.31	.23	.47	.41
Farmers	−.83	−.70	−.83	−.78

TABLE 8

Mean Swing to SPD 1965-1969 by Constituency Type

Constituency Type	Swing %		Number	
1. Metropolitan/white-collar	8.2		71	
a. Catholic		11.0		19
b. Protestant		9.0		26
c. Mixed		5.2		26
2. Urban-Industrial	4.6		105	
a. Catholic		6.4		26
b. Protestant		3.1		43
c. Mixed		5.2		36
3. Rural	3.7		72	
a. Catholic		3.8		40
b. Protestant		3.4		25
c. Mixed		4.2		7

In view of SPD gains in Catholic areas and in metropolitan seats, it should not be surprising that the largest swing to the Social Democrats took place in those Metropolitan/White-Collar seats that were also heavily Catholic. The data presented in Table 8 indicate that this was actually the case. The mean swing to the Social Democrats in 1969 was 11.0% in these 19 Catholic and Metropolitan districts. Over the 1961-1969 period, the mean SPD vote in these seats increased 11.1%, from 34.3% in 1961 to 45.4% in 1969. In Protestant-Metropolitan seats, the mean rise for this period was 6.8%. The SPD change Index in these constituencies was 116.1 as compared to 111.9 in the Protestant-Metropolitan districts and 107.7 in Mixed-Metropolitan seats.

Most of these SPD gains in the Catholic-Metropolitan areas appear to have been made at the expense of the Christian Democrats. The partial correlation between SPD and CDU change indices in these districts, controlling for the effects of the FDP and NPD poll, is −.77. In the Protestant and Mixed-Metropolitan seats, this relationship is considerably weaker, the partial coefficients in these two cases are −.12 and −.16.

In an attempt to bring into clearer focus the changes that have taken place in the relative impact of these demographic variables upon the SPD poll in the 1960s, a series of multiple stepwise regression and partial correlation analyses were carried out for the elections from 1961-1969. In the multiple regression analysis, both additive and multiplicative models were tested.

In the case of the Social Democrats as Table 9 shows, four variables—the percentage of Protestants, manual workers, white-collar employees (civil servants and *Angestellte*), and refugees—"explain" from 70 to 77% of the variance in the Social Democratic poll for the three Federal elections from 1961-1969. A "power function" or multiplicative model has little effect on the magnitude of this R^2 (Table 10).

Nonetheless, significant changes have taken place in the relative impact of these demographic variables upon the SPD vote. Above all, the explanatory power of the white-collar variable has increased significantly between 1961 and 1969. The partial r^2 for this variable (controlling for the effects of the Protestant, manual worker, and refugee variables) has risen from +.23 in 1961 to +.42 in 1969.[29] The Protestant component has declined slightly, while the partial r^2 for the manual worker variable has remained relatively constant especially between 1965 and 1969 (Table 11). The multiple correlation analysis revealed a somewhat similar pattern.[30] As Table 9 shows, the contribution to R^2 of the white-collar variable rose from 16.7% in 1961 to 41.2% in 1969. The decline in the contribution of the Protestant variable to R^2 was especially noticeable

TABLE 9
Ordered Cumulative Multiple Regression of SPD Vote
1961-1969

Step Number	Independent Variable	Cumulative R^2	Contribution of R^2
1961			
1	Protestants	.392	.392
2	White-collar and civil servants	.559	.167
3	Manual workers	.700	.141
4	Refugees	.713	.013
Total variance explained	71.3%		
1965			
1	White-collar and civil servants	.305	.305
2	Manual workers	.517	.212
3	Protestants	.680	.163
4	Refugees	.707	.027
Total variance explained	70.7%		
1969			
1	White-collar and civil servants	.412	.412
2	Protestants	.596	.184
3	Manual workers	.750	.154
4	Refugees	.770	.020
Total variance explained	77.0%		

TABLE 10
Comparison of the Square of the Multiple Correlation
Coefficient for Additive and Multiplicative
Models:[a] SPD Vote 1961-1969

	R^2					
	1961		**1965**		**1969**	
Multiple Predictors[b]	Additive	Multiplicative	Additive	Multiplicative	Additive	Multiplicative
White-collar and civil servants, manual workers, Protestants, refugees	.713	.670	.707	.672	.770	.721

a. The actual regression for the multiplicative model was: Log (Y) = Log (b) + m_1 Log (X_1) + m_2 Log (X_2) ... + m_n Log (X_n). The degrees of freedom for the SPD analysis is 243.

b. All variables are measured in percentages.

between 1961 and 1965 (39.2% to 16.3%); a similar pattern can be observed for the manual worker variable (Table 9). The refugee component has remained relatively weak over this period.

Not surprisingly, the partial correlation between the percentage of white-collar workers in a district and SPD vote also varies with the religious composition of the constituency (Table 12). This is consistent with the pattern of the party's vote and its simple demographic correlates.

Table 12 reports these partial r's for the most powerful correlates of the SPD vote by the religious composition of the 248 Bundestag districts. The white-collar variable for the 1961-1969 period was most "powerful" in the Catholic seats where it "explained" almost three-fourths of the variance in the 1969 SPD vote. In Protestant seats the partial r^2 for this variable is +.44 and in Mixed constituencies +.65.

The unusually high r^2 for the manual worker variable in Mixed constituencies (1969: +.67) in contrast to the Catholic (1969: +.25) or Protestant (1969: +.21) districts is a somewhat surprising finding that deserves further comment. What is perhaps at work here is the differentiating effect of the Catholic variable. We would hypothesize that the high SPD-manual worker correlation in Mixed seats is a function of increased support for the SPD in these heterogeneous districts from *Catholic workers*. Where Catholic workers, we would argue, are neither in a minority (Protestant seats), nor a majority (Catholic seats), the pressures from primary and especially secondary groups for supporting a "Catholic" party are less. The religious factor, in this context, is "cancelled out" and the Catholic manual worker is free to "vote his class." There is some, admittedly sketchy, support for this explanation. The correlation between the manual worker variable and the SPD vote, controlling for the effects of the Catholic variable, is higher in these Mixed seats than in the Catholic or Protestant districts. Indeed, in these latter two district types, a control for the Catholic variable has little effect on the SPD-manual worker correlation. In the case of the Mixed seats, however, the correlation rose in 1969 from +.47 to +.60 when we controlled for the Catholic variable.

2. Christian Democrats

Although the Christian Democrats' share of the 1969 poll declined by only 1.5%, the pattern of the party's decline has important implications for the future development of the West German party system. In direct district contests, the party lost 34 of its 153 direct Bundestag mandates and 20 of those 34 defeats were in cities over 100,000. In *Grosstaedten* (cities over 500,000) the Union lost all but two of the 12 district mandates

[28]

TABLE 11
Change and Continuity in Explanation/Prediction: Squares of Multiple and Partial Correlation Coefficients SPD Vote 1961-1969[a]

Predictor Variables	Partial r^2		
	1961	1965	1969
Protestants	.47	.38	.43
White-collar workers and civil servants	.23	.27	.42
Manual workers	.31	.39	.43
Refugees	.04	.07	.07
Multiple R^2	.71	.71	.77

a. Degrees of freedom for each coefficient = 243. The unit of analysis is the **Bundestagswahlkreis** (n=248). All variables are measured in percentages. Each predictor (independent) variable is related to the SPD vote with the effects of the other three variables simultaneously controlled.

TABLE 12
Squares of Partial Correlation Coefficients Between SPD Vote 1961-1969 and Various Demographic Variables by the Religious Composition of the District

Predictor Variables	District Type r^2		
	1961	1965	1969
Catholic (n=85)[a]			
Protestants	.47	.37	.42
White-collar and civil servants	.45	.61	.74
Manual workers	.16	.25	.25
Refugees	.00	.02	.02
Protestant (n=95)[b]			
Protestants	.10	.08	.12
White-collar and civil servants	.27	.25	.44
Manual workers	.19	.21	.21
Refugees	.08	.10	.10
Mixed (n=68)[c]			
Protestants	.21	.08	.04
White-collar and civil servants	.54	.61	.65
Manual workers	.65	.67	.67

a. Degrees of freedom for each coefficient = 80.

b. df = 90.

c. df = 63. See Note, Table 11.

it had held. The CDU now has direct mandates in only 13 urban areas, only one of which (Duesseldorf) is in the *Grosstadt* class.

The CDU vote, as pointed out above, declined most sharply in Metropolitan-Catholic seats (−4.8%, 1965-1969 Index: 90.2). The party also declined noticeably in Industrial-Catholic districts (−2.8%), Metropolitan, and Industrial-Mixed constituencies (−1.9%), and in Rural-Catholic seats (−1.8%). In all Protestant districts, however, the party's poll remained relatively stable; its mean vote in 1965 was 41.6%; in 1969, 41.4% (Index score 1965-1969: 99.2). Only in the Metropolitan-Protestant seats did the party decline noticeably (−1.7%, Index score: 95.6); in Industrial-Protestant seats the Union actually registered slight gains (.2%, Index score 100.8). Consistent with these results, the correlation between the Union's 1965-1969 *change Index* and the Protestant variable is significantly *positive*, r = +.28, (significant at .01 level) although the correlation between the *party's vote* and Protestant variable is strongly *negative*, 1969: r = −.58. Likewise, although the Catholic variable, as we shall see, is extremely powerful in explaining the variance in the CDU/CSU poll, this variable actually correlates negatively, r = −.23, with the party's 1965-1969 change Index. Thus, although CDU/CSU support still rests essentially on the Catholic factor, its impact over the 1965-1969 period has declined.

Our correlation analysis of the Christian Democratic vote reveals a clear trend toward ruralization. Between 1957 and 1969, for example, the correlation between the percentage of farmers in a district and the CDU poll rose from +.37 to +.74. Another indicator of ruralism, the percentage of independent nonmanuals (shopkeepers, artisans, and the like), in a district, also correlated progressively higher with the CDU vote over this period; from +.17 in 1957 to +.74 in 1969. As in the case of the Social Democrats, the religious component of the CDU/CSU vote has declined especially since 1961, nonetheless the simple correlation remains, even in 1969, quite substantial. Equally significant is the sharp rise in the negative correlations found between the CDU vote and the percentage of white-collar and manual workers in a district. Since 1957 the simple r between the manual worker variable and the CDU/CSU vote has dropped from +.07 to −.31; the r for the white-collar variable has likewise declined from −.26 in 1957 to −.58 at the September 1969 election (Table 13).

These findings indicate that Christian Democratic strength in the 1960s has receded to the rural and small-town districts of the Federal Republic. SPD strength in the heavily urban white-collar areas is indeed contrasted by the continued provincialization of the CDU.

TABLE 13
Main Demographic Correlates of CDU/CSU Vote 1957-1969[a]

Demographic Variable	1957	1961	1965	1969
Farmers in district	.37	.52	.68	.74
Independent nonmanuals in district	.17	.51	.66	.74
Catholics in district	.83	.83	.69	.66
Salaried nonmanuals in district	−.10	−.47	−.58	−.66
Population density of district	−.26	−.48	−.49	−.58
Manual workers in district	.07	−.20	−.30	−.31

a. See Note, Table 6.

Our multivariate analyses appear to confirm this trend. A stepwise regression of all demographic variables upon the Christian Democratic vote from 1961-1969 revealed three main components of the Union's poll: the percentage of Catholics, farmers, and independents in the district, and voting turnout in the respective election. As in the case of the Social Democrats, the total impact of these variables has remained remarkably constant; the R^2 in all three elections has ranged between 76% and 80% (Table 14). A multiplicative model produced R^2's that were actually

TABLE 14
Ordered Cumulative Multiple Regression of CDU/CSU Vote
1961-1969

Step Number	Independent Variable	Cumulative R^2	Contribution of R^2
1961			
1	Catholic	.683	.683
2	Farmers and independents	.787	.104
3	Turnout 1961	.805	.018
Total variance explained	80.5%		
1965			
1	Catholic	.482	.482
2	Farmers and independents	.755	.273
3	Turnout 1965	.763	.008
Total variance explained	76.3%		
1969			
1	Farmers and independents	.563	.563
2	Catholic	.783	.220
3	Turnout 1969	.791	.008
Total variance explained	79.1%		

consistently lower than those from the additive model (Table 15). Thus, the observation by Burnham and Sprague (1970: 489) that "the vote for more broadly based 'portmanteau' parties of a majority bent might display non-interactive characteristics similar to those associated with American major-party voting" appears to be substantiated in the case of the SPD and CDU/CSU.

But in spite of the constancy of the multiple correlation coefficient, the relative impact of these demographic variables has changed in a direction consistent with the simple correlates of the Union's poll enumerated above. What stands out in this analysis with remarkable clarity, using the partial correlation as a criterion, is the decline of the Catholic variable and the sharply increased importance of the ruralism variable.[32] The turnout variable has remained, especially after 1961, relatively unimportant. Although the Catholic variable explains, even in 1969, half the total variance in the CDU/CSU poll, this is considerably lower than the 71% of variance explained by this variable in 1961. The explanatory "power" of the farmer-independent nonmanual variable, on the other hand, has more than doubled between 1961 and 1969. The multiple regression analysis (Table 14) revealed, also, a decline in the contribution of the Catholic variable to R^2 and a sharp rise in the "rural" component of the CDU/CSU vote since the 1961 election. The contribution to R^2 of the farmer and independent nonmanual variable rose from 10.4% in 1961 to 56.3% by 1969 (Table 14).

This shift in the demographic composition of the Christian Democratic vote may mean that the traditional characterization of the Union as a broadly based "catch-all" party is in need of revision. Certainly these findings are not inconsistent with the reported decline in influence of the Catholic-labor wing of the party; a decline that is most notable in connection with the Union's recent pronouncements on the questions of Co-Determination and tax reform. The CDU/CSU has since the 1969 election in terms of policy become less of an "integrating party of the middle," the term once employed by former Chancellor Kiesinger to describe the party's role, and more of a conservative center-right party with a noticeable tendency to adopt a traditional nationalist stance on an increasing number of foreign policy issues.

The process of social-structural change underlying the relative impact of these party strategies and their effects on electoral outcomes can be discerned somewhat in the trend data on the composition of the work force presented in Table 17. The trends are clear and indeed are common to all advanced industrial societies:

TABLE 15

Comparison of the Square of the Multiple Correlation Coefficient
for Additive and Multiplicative Models:
CDU/CSU Vote 1961-1969[a]

	R^2					
	1961		1965		1969	
Multiple Predictors	Additive	Multiplicative	Additive	Multiplicative	Additive	Multiplicative
Catholics, farmers, and independent nonmanuals, turnout 1961-1969	.805	.680	.763	.656	.791	.749

a. Degrees of freedom = 244. All variables are measured in percentages.

(1) a steady decline in the percentage of the work force engaged in agriculture and independent nonmanual occupations;
(2) a steady increase in the white-collar sector of the work force;
(3) the stagnation of the manual worker and independent professional segments.

Our own analysis of the aggregate demographic and electoral data has shown quite clearly that Christian Democratic strength now lies in the static or declining sectors of the population, i.e. farmers, small shopkeepers, independent artisans. The cross-cutting effects of religion,

TABLE 16

Change and Continuity in Explanation/Prediction: Square of
Multiple and Partial Correlation Coefficients,
CDU/CSU Vote 1961-1969[a]

	Partial r^2		
Predictor Variables	1961	1965	1969
Catholics	.71	.53	.50
Farmers and independent nonmanuals	.16	.26	.34
Turnout 1961-1969	.09	.03	.04
Multiple R^2	.81	.76	.79

a. Degrees of freedom = 244. The unit of analysis is the **Bundestagswahlkreis** (n = 248). All variables are measured in percentages. See Note, Table 11.

however, still insure the Union a sizable segment of votes of Catholic manual workers and white-collar employees. Yet the continued secularization of West German society may well be cause for questioning the long-run future of any "religious" party.

In its concern with being "overtaken" on the right by the NPD and providing a new home for former FDP supporters, the Union appears in 1969 to have abandoned large areas of their nonmanual "middle" to the Social Democrats. Its nationalist foreign policy pronouncements failed to compensate for its inconsistent, defensive position on the D-Mark reevaluation and inflation issues, which were of greater salience to mass publics (Kaase, 1970).

B. THIRD PARTIES

1. Free Democrats

With only 5.8% of the vote and 30 Bundestag seats, the FDP suffered the worst defeat in its history. The extent of the party's decline (40% of its 1965 total vote) means that the voting behavior of 1965 Free Democratic supporters is probably of considerable importance in explaining changes in major party voting patterns. While a definitive answer to the question of the behavior of the FDP's former electorate must await the analysis of panel studies, a few tentative explorations with these aggregate data can be attempted.

The party's mean vote percentage declined by 4.2% in Protestant seats, 3.7% in religiously Mixed constituencies, and 2.9% in the 85 Catholic districts. When dividing the districts by the composition of the work force, it was found that the Free Democrats declined most shaply in Rural seats (4.2%), followed by the Industrial districts (3.7%), and the Metropolitan constituencies (3.3%). According to our combined occupation and religion classification scheme (Table 18) the FDP suffered its greatest drop in Rural-Protestant seats. In those 25 districts with over 30% of the work force in agricultural and independent nonmanual occupations and 60% or more of the inhabitants Protestant, the party's poll declined from 12.5% in 1965 to 6.6% in 1969, a drop of 5.9% which is considerably greater than its national decline of 3.7%.

The Free Democrats declined least in Catholic-Industrial districts and in religiously Mixed Industrial and Metropolitan constituencies. In these areas, however, the party in 1965 was already far below its national average and actually had little left to lose. Its best average poll (7.0%) was reached in the 26 Protestant-Metropolitan districts.

TABLE 17
**Changes in the Occupational Structure, 1950-1969 (in mean
percentages of total labor force for five-year intervals)**

	1950-1954 $\overline{X}$	1955-1959 $\overline{X}$	1960-1964 $\overline{X}$	1965-1969 $\overline{X}$
Farmers and independent nonmanuals	22.3	21.4	19.7	16.4
Manual workers	50.7	51.2	51.9	50.5
White-collar employees	24.9	25.5	26.5	31.2
Independent professionals	2.1	1.9	1.9	1.9
Total	100.0	100.0	100.0	100.0

SOURCE: Institut fuer Demoskopie, 1950-1954 (n=7): Study Nos. 040, 041, 050, 062, 066, 068, 074; 1955-1959 (n=10) Study Nos. 083, 089, 095, 1010, 1011, 1018, 1019, 1020, 1030, 1031; 1960-1964 (n=12): 1039, 1043, 1044, 1059, 1060, 1067, 1068, 1069, 1077, 1093, 1095, 1096; 1965-1969 (n=10): 1097, 1098, 2002, 2005, 2017, 2025, 2028, 2031, 2032, 2033. These data were made available through the Roper Public Opinion Research Center, Williamstown, Massachusetts.

Which of the major parties benefited most from this FDP decline? The partial correlation between the CDU and FDP change indices in Rural-Protestant seats, controlling for the effects of the SPD vote, is significantly negative (r = −.53), while that between the SPD and FDP indices (r = +.08) was insignificant (Table 19). The major party (SPD-CDU) correlation (r = −.32) in these seats, together with only average SPD gains, a relatively constant CDU/CSU vote, and a sharp FDP decline would seem to indicate that FDP losses were more beneficial to the CDU/CSU than to the Social Democrats. If the SPD did gain from FDP losses, the correlation between

TABLE 18
Mean FDP Decline 1965-1969 by District Type (in percentages)

District Type	Decline
Rural-Protestant	5.9
Industrial-Protestant	5.1
Rural-Mixed	4.3
Metropolitan-Protestant	4.1
Metropolitan-Catholic	3.7
Rural-Catholic	3.1
Industrial-Mixed	2.9
Metropolitan-Mixed	2.8
Industrial-Catholic	2.5
(Nationwide)	(3.7)

the SPD-FDP indices should be significantly negative; as Table 19 shows, it is not. The CDU/CSU, on the other hand, did apparently lose voters to the SPD, but the Union has been able to offset these losses with gains from former FDP supporters. A similar pattern, i.e. a sharp FDP decline, a constant CDU/CSU vote, slight SPD gains with, however significantly negative correlations between the FDP-CDU/CSU indices and the CDU/CSU-SPD indices, but not between the FDP-SPD change indices, is also evident in Protestant-Industrial seats and to a lesser extent, in Protestant-Metropolitan constituencies.[33]

Not surprisingly although the FDP vote for all elections correlates highly with the Protestant variable, this is not the case for the party's 1965-1969 change Index, which is actually significantly *negatively* correlated with the Protestant variable ($r = -.20$ significant at the .01 level). The correlation between the FDP's change Index and the Catholic variable, however, is significantly positive ($r = +.16$, significant at the .05 level). This contrasts with the consistently strong negative relationship found in all elections between the Catholic variable and the FDP vote. This pattern indicates that the aggregate FDP decline was indeed centered more in Protestant than in Catholic constituencies.

The apparent CDU/CSU exploitation of former FDP support represents the continuation of a trend that has been evident in national elections since 1953. On the basis of a secondary analysis of survey data collected over the past decade, the German political sociologist Klaus Liepelt and his associates (1968b) found that the CDU/CSU has benefited the most from

TABLE 19
Partial Correlations Between Party Change Indices in
Protestant Constituencies

Constituency Type	Partial r CDU, FDP:SPD	Partial r FDP, SPD:CDU	Partial r SPD, CDU:FDP
Rural-Protestant (n=25)	−.53[a]	+.08	−.32[c]
Metropolitan-Protestant (n=27)	−.51[a]	−.22[c]	+.02
Industrial-Protestant (n=43)	−.45[b]	−.03	−.33[c]
All Protestant seats (n=95)	−.56[a]	−.09	−.21[c]

a. Significant at .001 level.
b. Significant at .01 level.
c. Significant at .05 level.

the decline of the third and minor party vote; the Union has tended to gain twice as much from small parties such as the Free Democrats and the now extinct German Party (DP) and Refugee Party (BHE). The Social Democratic gains over the 1957-1969 period, on the other hand, have come predominantly from former CDU/CSU supporters and previous nonvoters. Among FDP voters surveyed between 1964 and 1967, for example, Liepelt (1968a: Table 5) found that 46% had previously voted for the CDU/CSU, while only 16% of FDP supporters in this period had a prior history of support for the SPD. Also, FDP adherents during this period preferred the CDU over the SPD as their second choice by a ratio of 2.4 : 1.[34]

In past elections, expecially those of 1961 and 1965, the FDP could count on substantial support from voters who in policy terms generally preferred the Union, but who voted FDP as a limited means of censuring the CDU without, however, inducing a *Machtwechsel*, i.e. an SPD government. Support for the party was one way of protesting against certain CDU policies and/or leaders such as Adenauer and Strauss without deserting the middle-class camp. Thus, for a segment of Germany's bourgeois electorate the party became a vehicle for limited protest. The first choice of these electors, however, remained the CDU/CSU and the condition for their support of the Free Democrats was that the party renew its coalition with the Union.[35]

According to surveys conducted by Klingemann and Pappi (1970: 121), roughly 40% of the party's electorate in 1961 and 1965 was composed of voters who in the preceding election (1957 or 1961) had supported the CDU/CSU. In 1969, however, only 18% of the FDP's vote came from 1965 CDU/CSU supporters. Also, according to one panel study (reported in Klingemann and Pappi, 1969) conducted in September and November of 1969, the FDP had lost 34% of its 1965 electorate to the CDU in 1969. Between 1957 and 1961 and between 1961 and 1965, movements from the CDU/CSU to the FDP accounted for 33% and 21% of all party switching. In 1969, however, the CDU/CSU-FDP path accounted for only 6% of all movements (Klingemann and Pappi, 1970).

This loss of votes from traditional supporters of a bourgeois CDU-FDP alliance can be traced above all to the FDP's increasing inclination to support the Social Democrats, the most dramatic manifestation of which was the Heinemann election. After March 1969, the orientation of CDU/CSU voters toward the FDP became increasingly negative (Zentralarchiv Data Pool, 1969).[36] Also, by the spring of 1969, FDP identifiers were closer to SPD supporters on domestic issues such as tax and education reform than they were to CDU/CSU supporters.

An analysis of the simple correlates of the FDP vote over the last four elections revealed few consistent trends in the demographic pattern of the party's support. However, our partial correlation analysis did reveal certain changes. As Table 20 indicates, the importance of the Protestant variable has declined steadily between 1961 and 1969; the partial r^2 for this variable has dropped from +.33 in 1961 to +.23 in 1969. The importance of the white-collar variable, as in the case of the Social Democratic vote, has increased; the partial r^2 between this variable and the FDP vote rose from +.33 in 1961 and 1965 to +.40 for the September 1969 election. Also one measure of urbanization, the percentage of constituency residents in multiple-unit dwellings, increased in importance between 1961 and 1969, although the 1969 partial r^2 (+.21) is slightly lower than the 1965 figure (+.24). As in the case of the other parties, the refugee variable, regardless of the mode of analysis, remains relatively unimportant.

But in spite of changes in the relative importance of various demographic variables, these aggregate materials still indicate that, on the whole, the FDP remains a predominantly middle-class, urban, and Protestant party. These findings are generally supported by survey data (Klingemann and Pappi, 1970). Although in terms of political orientations and opinions, the post-1969 FDP electorate is much more supportive of a liberal, progressive course in domestic and foreign policies and also supports the present coalition with the SPD, the social-structural characteristics of its electorate have remained relatively constant throughout the 1960s.[37]

TABLE 20
Change and Continuity in Explanation/Prediction: Squares of
Multiple and Partial Correlation Coefficients,
FDP Vote 1961-1969

Predictor Variables	Partial r^{2a}		
	1961	1965	1969
Protestants	.33	.28	.23
White-collar workers and civil servants	.33	.33	.40
Multiple-unit dwellings	.15	.24	.21
Refugees	.01	.00	.04
Multiple R^2	.55	.50	.51

a. Degrees of freedom = 244. All variables are measured in percentages. The unit of analysis is the **Bundestagswahlkreis** (n=248). See Note, Table 11.

TABLE 21

**Partial Correlations Between NPD Change Index 1965-1969
and Those of Bundestag Parties (SPD, CDU/CSU, FDP)
by District Type[a]**

	District Type	SPD	CDU/CSU	FDP
1.	Metropolitan-Catholic	+.12	−.14	+.26
2.	Metropolitan-Protestant	+.78	−.36	+.44
3.	Metropolitan-Mixed	−.47	−.84	+.63
4.	Industrial-Catholic	+.01	−.25	+.35
5.	Industrial-Protestant	−.19	−.30	+.39
6.	Industrial-Mixed	−.16	−.68	+.40
7.	Rural-Catholic	+.22	−.32	+.24
8.	Rural-Protestant	−.22	+.19	−.25
9.	Rural-Mixed	+.72	+.34	−.88

a. The effects of the third and fourth party indices are always controlled.

2. National Democrats

The emergence of the NPD as a significant national political force
coincided with the fall of the Erhard government and the establishment of
the Grand Coalition in December 1966. Founded in 1964 from remnants
of the outlawed *Deutsche Reichspartei* and other smaller nationalist
organizations, it had since 1966 secured representation in seven state
parliaments averaging roughly 7% of the party vote.[38] But with 4.3% of
the poll in 1969 it failed to clear the 5% hurdle necessary for Bundestag
representation, nor did the NPD match its earlier performances in state
elections. Nonetheless, it did receive more votes than any other conservative, nationalist party since 1957.

TABLE 22

Main Demographic Correlates of NPD Vote 1965-1969[a]

	1965	1966-1968 State Elections[b]	1969
Independent nonmanuals in district	.19	.36	.40
Farmers in district	.12	.33	.32
Protestants in district	.39	.28	.29

a. See Note, Table 6.
b. Hesse, Bavaria, Lower Saxony, Rheinland Palatinate, Schleswig-Holstein, Bremen,
Baden-Wuerttemberg.

Nationally, the NPD's vote correlates negatively albeit weakly with both the CDU/CSU (r = −.02) and SPD (r = −.18) poll. There is a moderately positive relationship (r = +.24) between the NPD vote and that of the Free Democrats. This latter relationship declines, somewhat, however, when we control for the effects of the Protestant factor; the partial correlation between the NPD and FDP controlling for the Protestant variable is +.16.

In examining the correlation between the NPD change Index and those of the Bundestag parties in our nine district types (Table 21), it appears that the NPD was most competitive with the Christian Democrats. With the exception of the Rural-Protestant and Rural-Mixed constituencies, the correlation between NPD and CDU/CSU change indices, controlling for the effects of the SPD and FDP vote, is consistently negative. In the former two cases, both parties (NPD and CDU/CSU) appear to have profited from the sizable FDP losses in Rural constituencies. There was, it would seem, a competition between these parties for the support of the same groups of voters. This competition was most intense in the religiously Mixed-Industrial and Metropolitan seats followed by Protestant-Metropolitan and Rural-Catholic districts.

The NPD vote correlates most strongly with the percentage of independent nonmanuals, farmers, Protestants, and working women in a district. This latter variable could also be considered an indicator of "ruralism"; it is moderately correlated with the farmer (+.19) and independent nonmanual variables (+.30). There is also a positive correlation between the NPD poll and the percentage of refugees in a district. This relationship has sharply declined, however, between 1965 (the first year that the party contested a Federal election) and 1969 (Table 22).

When controlling for the Protestant variable, the 1965 correlation between the NPD vote and the percentage employed in agricultural occupations rises from +.12 to +.22; for the 1969 poll the partial r, controlling for the percentage of Protestants, increases from +.32 to +.41. Not surprisingly, then, the NPD secured its highest average poll (6.0%) in the Rural-Protestant constituencies. The party also came very close (4.9%) to surmounting the 5% hurdle in the 43 Protestant-Industrial districts and the seven Mixed-Rural seats.

As in the case of the three Bundestag parties, the NPD vote was analyzed through the application of both multiple regression and partial correlation analysis. A multiple regression analysis of the NPD vote enabled us to explain only 36% of the variance in the party's poll for both 1965 and 1969 using a standard additive model. This contrasts sharply with the 70 to 80% of variance that can be explained in the major party

TABLE 23

Change and Continuity in Explanation/Prediction: Squares of
Multiple and Partial Correlation Coefficients,
NPD Vote 1965-1969

Predictor Variables[b]	Partial r^{2a}	
	1965 (mult.)[c]	1969 (mult.)
Farmers and independent nonmanuals	.03 (.10)	.17 (.23)
Protestants	.16 (.20)	.18 (.20)
Women in work force	.16 (.13)	.07 (.04)
Refugees	.06 (.06)	.01 (.01)
Multiple R^2	.36 (.44)	.36 (.40)

a. Degrees of freedom = 244. See Note, Table 11.

b. All variables are measured in percentages. The unit of analysis is the **Bundestags-wahldreis** (n = 248).

c. With multiplicative model.

(SPD and CDU) vote with these ecological variables; the FDP R^2 of 50-55% is between these two extremes.

The relative impact of these variables has, however, varied somewhat between the elections of 1965 and 1969. The partial correlation analysis reported in Table 23 revealed a sharp increase in the explanatory power of the farmer, independent nonmanual variable between 1965 and 1969 (3% to 17%), while the effects of the Protestant variable have remained relatively constant.

TABLE 24

Comparison of the Square of the Multiple Correlation Coefficient
for Additive and Multiplicative Models:
NPD Vote 1965-1969

Multiple Predictors[a]	R^2			
	1965		1969	
	Additive	Multiplicative	Additive	Multiplicative
Protestants, farmers and independent nonmanuals, refugees, percentage women in work force	.358	.441	.362	.400

a. All variables are measured in percentages. Degrees of freedom = 243.

In the case of the National Democrats, however, the employment of a multiplicative model did yield results generally consistent with the hypothesis that:

> voting for radical parties (whether of the left or right) is an act of positive or aggressive alienation; that such alienation is linked to feelings which are part of a class of involuntary responses; that it may well be that a (multiplicative) power function is the general form of relationship between the magnitude of stimuli and of non-voluntary responses; and that one might cousequently expect to find . . . that correlations based on an additive theoretical model explain substantially less of the variance in the radical vote than do correlations based on a multiplicative theoretical model [Burnham and Sprague, 1970: 471].

A power function model does indeed explain more of the variance in the National Democratic vote for 1965 and 1969 than the additive model (Table 24), yet the increases, 8.3% in 1965 and 3.8% in 1969 are hardly spectacular. These findings are certainly suggestive, however, and should be pursued in future work with aggregate data. In the case of the NPD, analyses of the party's vote in state elections during the 1966-1969 period with a smaller unit of analysis might yield results more consistent with the Soares-Hamblin argument.

IV. CONCLUDING REMARKS

The analysis of the demographic correlates of the parties' poll has clearly shown that SPD gains over the 1957-1969 period have been based in large part on the party's increased support in Catholic and middle-class districts. Most of these gains appear to have been made at the expense of the Christian Democrats, but the Union has been able to offset these losses somewhat with gains from the Free Democrats and other now extinct small parties. This pattern was most discernible in the following district types: Protestant and Mixed-Metropolitan districts, all Industrial seats, and Rural-Protestant constituencies. The FDP, which lost votes to the Christian Democrats in all constituencies, was able to offset its losses somewhat by gains from the Social Democrats in the Metropolitan-Catholic and Industrial-Mixed seats. Finally in the Rural constituencies the Christian Democrats and FDP also lost some support to the National Democrats.

There is also some evidence that the combined SPD-FDP electorate in 1969 constituted a genuine "ideological" majority which gave the two parties a mandate, albeit slim, to form a government without the Christian Democrats. According to the panel study conducted by the Institut fuer Demoskopie (1970), 51% of the FDP's 1969 voters when reinterviewed in October 1969 before the formal investiture of the Brandt government, preferred a coalition with the Socialists, 32% supported an alignment with the CDU/CSU, and 17% were undecided. The sample of all ballots taken by the Federal Statistical Office in 1971 showed that two-thirds of those FDP voters who split their ballot in 1969, that is who voted for the party on the second (party list) part of the ballot, but not on the first (district candidate) part preferred the SPD over the Christian Democrats.[39] This was a sharp reversal from the 1965 pattern when FDP voters who split their ballot preferred the CDU/CSU to the SPD by almost a 3-1 margin. In some states even more dramatic changes took place. In Hamburg, for example, the percentage of FDP voters giving their district vote to the SPD candidate increased from 8.5% in 1965 to 48.7% in 1969. Even in Lower Saxony, where the FDP has traditionally been more closely identified with the CDU/CSU, the percentage of FDP supporters splitting their ballots in favor of the Social Democrats rose from 5.8% in 1965 to 23.2% in 1969 (Kaase, 1970: 49).

A. THE FUTURE OF THE PARTY SYSTEM

The demographic structure of the Christian Democratic vote shows an increasing ruralization and provincialization inconsistent with the party's self-image as an "integrating party of the middle." Although still Germany's largest and most successful party, the Union must in future elections seek to regain the support it once enjoyed in urban-metropolitan areas if it is to maintain parity with the Social Democrats. The third and minor-party electoral reservoir, so profitably tapped by the Union in earlier elections, is almost exhausted.

Yet ironically this CDU/CSU decline has not produced a shift in internal party equilibrium in favor of the Union's more progressive elements. The influence of the conservative Catholic-agrarian wing, centered in the South and Southwest, has grown in the postelection period because of the party's successive gains in state elections held since 1969. But these electoral gains have been largely the result of the Union's "mopping-up" the remnants of the NPD and the "old," conservative FDP (Wildenmann, 1970: 15; Kaiser, 1971: 5). If our analysis is correct these electoral successes will be short-lived, but their major long-range effect may be to weaken the progressive wing of the party to the point where it would take a series of decisive national defeats to return the CDU/CSU to a more center position. This implies, of course, that the campaign of 1973 and perhaps of 1977 will be characterized by a greater degree of polarization between the major parties than was the case throughout the 1960s.

The Social Democrats, in spite of electoral gains, are still faced with the dual problem of maintaining their newly won support in middle-class areas, without thereby alienating its left wing. The changes in the party's policies, tactics, leadership, and style that have been especially noticeable since the late 1950s and subsumed under the general strategy of "embracing the middle," have not occurred without internal opposition especially from the party's new and old Left. The SPD Left has argued that the party by "embracing the middle" has in fact adapted to the economic and sociological givens of West Germany and has essentially taken the easy road to political power. The party's entrance into the Grand Coalition and its 1969 alignment with the middle-class Free Democrats are cited as evidence that the party has sacrificed its principles and commitment to social and political change. Instead of attempting to convince the electorate of the need for an extensive restructuring of the economy and society, the party has restricted itself to the function of representing diverse social groupings without thereby changing the power relationships between them. The Left's *bete noire* in this regard is Schiller who has steadfastly refused to consider programs such as steeper inheritance taxes and an extension of Co-Determination.

In terms of internal party equilibrium, however, there is little doubt that the election results strengthened and consolidated the position of the party's moderate "Establishment," i.e., that group within the SPD drawn largely from the ranks of party functionaries and office holders at local, state, and national levels who conceive of the SPD as a center-left, yet broadly based party of reform. The classic "proletarian core" of the party, still based in some trade unions has been in continuous decline since the 1950s and the 1969 election, to the extent that it justified the Grand Coalition and indeed the entire Brandt-Wehner strategy, weakened it still further. In the future the most significant intraparty opposition to the present course will come from the party's new Left, largely centered in the SPD's youth organizations. This group conceives of itself as the SPD of the 1980s and supplements its class conflict pronouncements with a vigorous generational struggle (Zundel, 1970). Its ranks appear to be growing; between 1960 and 1969 the percentage of new SPD members under 30 rose from 27.5% to 47.6%.[40] Although weakly represented in the party's national leadership bodies, i.e., Federal Praesidium and Executive, the Young Socialists have become increasingly active and influential in the party's local organizations where they capitalize on the relative inactivity of the rank and file (Diederich, 1968). To the extent that the national success of the party has increased their own notoriety, the Young Socialists since 1969 have profited from a strategy they in principle opposed.

1. Stability of the Bipartite Pattern

Although the two-party share of the popular vote now approaches 90%, there are still grounds for caution about any predictions as to the future direction and stability of the party system. First, as numerous studies of German electoral psychology have shown, there is considerable latent partisanship among German voters.[41] According to surveys conducted by Kaase and Wildenmann in 1967, only 54% of the electorate are moderate to strong supporters of a political party. This is considerably lower than the American party identification level of 75 to 80%. In a 1969 survey, also conducted by Kaase and Wildenmann, a national sample when asked whether they were "convinced supporters" of a particular party or whether they did not feel attached *(verbunden)* to a party, gave responses that support the latent partisanship argument; only 28.9% indicated that they were convinced supporters *(ueberzeugte Anhaenger)* of a party.[42]

In addition the relatively low levels of affective feelings about the political system, the reluctance to reveal the "self" in the political sphere (Plog, 1963; Scheuch et al., 1969) and the low levels of participation in political and quasi-political organizations all point to a latent partisanship that could be triggered by crisis or near-crisis situations and channeled into support for new surge parties.

It is also still difficult to interpret the concentration of support for the major parties as an expression of the electorate's desire for party government on the Anglo-American model. Numerous surveys have indicated that the majority of the electorate has no clear conception as to the primary responsibilities of the governing and opposition parties in a parliamentary system. For example, in a 1967 study, 80% of a national sample agreed that a strong parliamentary opposition was important, yet 77% of the same group expressed from moderate to enthusiastic support of the Grand Coalition (Wildenmann and Schleth, 1968: 21-22). These contradictory sentiments—abstract support for a strong opposition coupled with favorable orientations towards a Grand Coalition—were also found in earlier studies of the electorate's conception of the party system. An EMNID Institut (1961: 1-3) study revealed, for example, that 40% of a national sample agreed with the statement: "it would not be good for the country if one party had 50% or more of the votes because then its power would be too great." In a 1964 survey only 13% of the respondents expressed a preference for one-party government on the English model. Almost two-thirds of the sample preferred a government composed of two or more parties (Eberlein, 1968: 103).

A further obstacle to responsible majority party government lies in the structure of the major parties. The key component in the postwar German party system, the Christian Democratic Union, remains a loosely structured, heterogeneous movement which has yet to stand the test of an extended period of opposition. Whether the Union can hold together without national political power is one of the most intriguing questions of German politics.

The CDU/CSU has, for the most part, been successful in bringing together diverse religious, regional, class, and ideological interests into a broadly based "catch-all" party. But it is sometimes forgotten that the Bavarian wing of the movement, the Christian Social Union, is a self-contained political organization with its own traditions, leadership, and style. It merges with the CDU only in Bonn, where its Bundestag deputies constitute a solid bloc tightly disciplined by the party's leadership.

The CSU actually has stronger traditions and a greater sense of identity than the national Union. It is the postwar successor to the Bavarian Peoples Party (BVP), which was the strongest party in Bavaria during the interwar period. Indeed, throughout modern Bavarian political history, a rural, small-town Catholic party has been the strongest political force in the state.[43] Like its predecessors, the CSU is overwhelmingly Catholic; 90% of its 80,000 members are Catholic and the largest single occupational group in its membership is the Catholic clergy. Moreover the CSU, unlike the national Union, has no labor wing, its strongest support comes from nonmanuals in rural and small towns.[44]

The CSU and especially its leader, Franz Josef Strauss, have adopted policy positions that increasingly diverge from those of the CDU. In foreign policy the CSU has consistently pressed for a maintenance of a "hard line" posture toward the Communist countries. It has opposed (1) the abandonment or even revision of the Hallstein doctrine, (2) the nuclear nonproliferation treaty, and (3) the normalization of relations with Eastern Europe. It was largely because of CSU pressure that the Christian Democrats refused to support the SPD's pleas for a bipartisan approach to the negotiations with the Soviet Union and Poland. In domestic policy the CSU, devoid of a Catholic-labor wing, has also opposed some rather liberal CDU plans for Co-Determination, education, and tax reform. Since the

CSU and Strauss play a key role in national leadership selection, possessing at least veto power, the probabilities for conflict between the Bavarian wing of the Union and the less conservative, "reformist" elements of the party centered in the large urban areas of the West and North will increase with the continuance of the Union's opposition role in Bonn.[45]

Also, although the Social Democrats made impressive gains for the fourth straight election, it remains to be seen whether the 1969 performance, which rested in large part upon gains among Catholic white-collar workers and skilled manual workers, can be maintained and extended in future elections. If the SPD is to become a broadly based national party it must also still make inroads into the Union's strong position in the Catholic and rural areas of South and Southwest Germany. Specifically in the *Laender* of Baden-Wuerttemberg and Bavaria, which together constitute a third of the electorate, the party remains weak. Its share of the party vote in these two states is only slightly above the 35% mark and even in 1969 the party was able to win only 19 of 79 district contests (23%). It thus remains, in spite of its overall national performance, a distinctly minority party in the South and Southwest. And even in the state of Nordrhein-Westfalen, which contains almost another third of the total national electorate, the SPD's 1969 performance represented more of a consolidation of gains made at the 1966 state election than a breakthrough to a solid majority. Indeed at the June 1970 state elections in Nordrhein-Westfalen the Social Democrats dropped back to their pre-1966 level.[46]

Thus in spite of the new bipartite structure of the party system, the attitudinal and demographic remnants of the unstable multiparty pattern can still be discerned. The institutionalization of a posttotalitarian regime is a process that still continues in the Federal Republic.

APPENDIX A
Party Vote in Federal Elections, 1949-1969 (2nd ballot)
(in percentages)

Year	1949	1953	1957	1961	1965	1969
Turnout	78.5	86.0	87.8	87.7	86.9	86.8
CDU/CSU	31.0	45.2	50.2	45.3	47.6	46.1
SPD	29.2	28.8	31.8	36.2	39.3	42.7
FDP	11.9	9.5	7.7	12.8	9.5	5.8
Others	27.9	17.5	10.3	5.7	3.6	5.4
Total	100.0	100.0	100.0	100.0	100.0	100.0

APPENDIX B
Demographic Characteristics of Constituency Types

	Metropolitan (71)	Industrial (105)	Rural (72)	Nationwide
Density (inhabitants per sq. km.)	2,357.4	629.5	117.9	236.5
Percentage				
Refugee	20.7	22.3	20.6	21.3
Protestant	53.4	52.5	43.5	50.1
Catholic	39.3	43.8	54.5	45.6
Farmer	1.5	6.6	18.3	8.5
Independent nonmanual	9.2	11.4	16.9	12.4
Civil servant	6.0	4.2	4.0	4.6
White-collar	32.2	19.5	13.7	21.4
Manual worker	43.3	50.5	40.8	45.6
Women in the work force	33.6	32.0	33.7	33.0
In multiple-unit dwellings	75.0	43.6	26.2	47.5

NOTES

1. The election was the subject of an entire issue of Comparative Politics (1970). In addition, Werner Kaltefleiter and his associates at the University of Cologne have produced a volume on the election in the Verfassung und Verfassungswirklichkeit series edited by Ferdinand A. Hermens (see Kaltefleiter et al., 1970). Both survey and aggregate data are analyzed in Kaase (1970) and Klingemann and Pappi (1970). The Klingemann-Pappi analysis was also published in English in the special Comparative Politics issue.

2. In addition to publishing basic demographic data by constituency, the Federal Statistical Office has, since 1953, been authorized to include questions identifying the age and sex of the voter on about 2% of all ballots. This very large random sample (1969 n=828,000) gives us very accurate information on the age and sex distributions of the party vote. For a useful listing of available German aggregate electoral data see Diederich (1969).

3. The works by Kaase (1970) and Klingemann and Pappi (1970) are, to my knowledge, the only studies that have employed extensive correlation analyses with these data. With the development of modern data processing facilities at German universities this situation will hopefully change.

4. This election was the subject of the first major West German voting and election study (Hirsch-Weber and Schuetz, 1957).

5. This stress on the security theme employed by both major parties was based in part on the results of numerous opinion surveys which consistently revealed that job and personal security were the prime concerns of mass publics. This has been

confirmed in a recent cross-national study (Katona et al., 1971: 125-127). When asked what they regarded as the most important consideration in selecting an occupation, 70% of a German national sample stated that "economic security" was the most important factor. In the United States, Britain, and the Netherlands, the percentage mentioning economic security was 34%, 33%, and 31% respectively; personal fulfillment and development were rated higher in these latter cultures. In the West German sample, this concern for economic security does not decline when controlling for education or occupation. In the other cultures studied, however, job security became less salient with rising occupational status. In the German case, we are dealing then with what is apparently a relatively stable cultural trait.

6. Postelection surveys (Institut fuer Demoskopie, 1970: 147-152), however, indicated that the strikes were not as salient as some campaign observers had assumed.

7. See Kaase (1970: 63, 69) for 1969 survey data on this point. Similar findings from different sources are reported in *Die Zeit,* June 13, 1969: 35. A recent comparative study which also documents this point is Katona et al. (1971).

8. In a 1969 survey, when asked who was most responsible for the improvement in the economic situation, 33% of a national sample named Schiller, 15% the Grand Coalition, 14% Strauss, 11% Kiesinger, 11% the SPD, 11% the CDU/CSU, 3% Willy Brandt and 2% gave no answer (Kaase, 1970: 68).

9. According to one study, 45% of a national sample when asked who had better judgment in this area named Schiller, 21% Strauss, 13% Kiesinger, and 21% gave no answer (Kaase, 1970: 68).

10. For an account of the SPD's 1961 campaign, see Merkl (1962). The 1965 campaign is succinctly analyzed by Kaltefleiter (1966).

11. For a summary of these poll data see Institut fuer Demoskopie (1965: 290-291; 1968: 215ff.)

12. Surveys conducted since Brandt's investiture do indeed show a rise in his popularity among 1969 CDU/CSU voters and a resultant decline in support for Kiesinger.

13. The role of the electoral law issue in the politics of coalition formation and maintenance is discussed in Conradt (1970).

14. See also Schmidt's remark at the SPD Parteitag in April 1969, in Protokoll, SPD Parteitag (1969: 64-65).

15. See the interview with the FDP's National Chairman Walter Scheel, in Der Spiegel (1969a, 32: 26ff) for a statement of FDP election goals.

16. According to surveys conducted between September 10 and September 17, 1969, 49% of FDP supporters preferred a coalition with the Social Democrats, while 29% wanted an alignment with the CDU/CSU and 11% preferred a renewal of the Grand Coalition. The remaining FDP supporters were undecided (The Times, September 1969). Similar findings were reported by researchers at the Zentralarchiv in Cologne (Sueddeutsche Zeitung, 1969).

17. The *Jungdemokraten,* the party's major youth organization, threatened to leave the party if a coalition with the CDU/CSU were formed. Surveys of new (i.e., post-1966) FDP supporters also found a strong preference for a coalition with the Social Democrats and an essentially negative orientation toward the CDU/CSU.

18. According to some surveys, the FDP by early 1969 was also gaining more support from former SPD voters than from one-time CDU supporters (see Zundel, 1969a: 4).

19. In nine nationwide surveys conducted between February 1968 and April 1969, the percentage of respondents with a negative orientation toward the Grand Coalition ranged from 23.2% in October 1968, to 39% in March 1969; the mean percentage for this period was 29.6%. The percentage of these respondents who then indicated that voting for the FDP was the best means of expressing dissatisfaction with the coalition ranged from 23.5% in November 1968, to 30.3% in February 1969; the mean percentage was 26.2% (Zentralarchiv Data Pool, 1969).

20. Panel surveys conducted by the DIVO organization for the Zentralarchiv at Cologne University showed that in the last three weeks of the campaign 25% of those respondents intending to vote FDP actually supported the Christian Democrats on September 29. In all, only 42% of those respondents, who three weeks before the election intended to vote FDP actually supported the party (see Klingemann and Pappi, 1969: 2).

21. This point is also made in the postmortem of the election written by Willy Weyer, the FDP's Chairman in Nordrhein-Westfalen (Weyer, 1970). In state elections held since the formation of the SPD-FDP government, the Free Democrats have been most successful, i.e. in Hesse and Bavaria, where they have clearly stated at the outset of the campaign their preference for a coalition partner.

22. After this disaster, several SPD members of the Kiesinger cabinet, including Willy Brandt, considered resigning from the government in order to devote full time to mending the party's internal divisions and preparing for the 1969 campaign.

23. The classification of districts into Catholic, Protestant, and Mixed was based on the religious composition of the district as reported in the 1950 and 1961 Census. Catholic and Protestant seats are simply those in which 60% or more of the population belong to one of the confessions; Mixed seats are those in which no one religion reaches this level. By this scheme, 85 of the 248 districts are "Catholic," 95 "Protestant," and 68 "Mixed." With the 1957 data, 91 districts were classified as Catholic, 105 as Protestant, and 51 as Mixed.

24. The party change Index for 1965-1969 was simply:

$$\text{Index} = \frac{\text{Party Vote 1969} \cdot \text{Turnout 1965}}{\text{Party Vote 1965} \cdot \text{Turnout 1969}} \cdot 100$$

The second (party list) ballot total was used for the computation of the Index. It is the same Index employed by Hirsch-Weber and Schuetz (1957: 431) and by Klingemann and Pappi (1970: 526).

25. According to aggregate data for the 1949-1957 period analyzed by the Institut fuer angewandte Sozialwissenschaft (1969: 20) there was no clear trend of increased support for the SPD in Catholic areas between 1949 and 1953 or 1953 and 1957.

26. By "swing" we mean simply the percentage difference between the CDU/CSU and SPD in 1969 minus the percentage difference between the two parties in 1965.

27. Unfortunately, the age and sex distributions for each Bundestag constituency have not been published by the Federal Statistical Office since 1957. Thus, these variables could not be included in our correlation analysis of the elections from 1961-1969. Although significant differences in party support between male and female voters and between different age groups have been reported (Statistisches Bundesamt, 1971), most survey analysts have found them to largely disappear when

controls for religion and social class are applied (Klingemann and Pappi, 1970; Kaase, 1970). In the case of the sex variable, preliminary analyses by the author of surveys conducted between 1950 and 1970 by the Institut fuer Demoskopie indicate that the greater support by women for the Christian Democrats is basically a function of higher religiousity among Catholic females. However, more extensive research on the age variable, particularly through generational or cohort analysis of the type employed by Butler and Stokes (1969) with British data, is definitely needed.

28. See Soares and Hamblin (1967) and Burnham and Sprague (1970) for two recent studies which employ multiplicative models in the analysis of aggregate data. Our analysis differs from these studies in its use of trend data and its examination of the votes for all major parties.

29. Each partial r^2 between the predictor (independent) variable and the party vote was computed with simultaneous controls for the effects of the other independent variables. Thus, in the case of the SPD vote from 1961-1969 where four variables were found to be most powerful, the effects of the three other independent variables were always controlled when computing the partial correlation coefficients reported in Table 11.

30. In the multiple regression analysis, a stepwise condensation procedure was used which eliminated variables one at a time in an order inverse to their t-values. The regression analysis was repeated until the beta coefficients of the remaining independent variables were significantly different from zero at the .05 level. In the case of the SPD, we were left with the white-collar, Protestant, manual worker and refugee variables. In the analysis of the CDU/CSU vote, only three variables remained: the Catholic, farmer independent nonmanual, and turnout variables. Since these demographic variables are not completely independent of one another, we cannot assume that the stepwise increases in R^2 are an indicator of relative potency of effect. They do, of course, indicate what proportion of the unexplained variance is accounted for by a new variable. However, it should be noted that the pattern found in the multiple regression analysis is quite consistent with the results of the partial correlation analysis.

31. For a recent contextual analysis with state *(Land)* data, see Harder and Pappi (1970).

32. As in the case of the SPD vote, each partial r^2 between the independent variable (Catholic, farmer-independent, and turnout) and the CDU/CSU vote from 1961-1969 was computed with controls for the effects of the two other independent variables. The same procedure was also followed for the analysis of the FDP and the NPD vote.

33. In state elections held since the 1969 Federal Election, this trend seems to have continued. In Nordrhein-Westfalen, Lower Saxony, and Hesse, for example, the party's vote declined most drastically in the rural Protestant regions with the CDU apparently profiting most from this drop in support. The party apparently gained new voters, however, among white-collar voters in large urban areas. In Hesse, for example, the correlation (Pearson's r) between the FDP vote and the percentage of white-collar workers in a district increased sharply from +.14 in 1966 to +.81 in 1970.

34. Liepelt's analysis of FDP voting was based on an n of 1391. In the 1969 election, as pointed out below, this pattern of the FDP voter's second choice was sharply reversed. See also Liepelt (1970) for a comparative analysis employing both German and Austrian data.

35. It is, thus, not surprising that opinion polls have consistently underestimated the FDP vote since in past elections up to half of the party's actual supporters did not finally decide to vote FDP until a few days before the election (Bluecher, 1962: 69).

36. Party orientation was measured through a Skalometer with which the respondent was asked to rate each party on a scale ranging from −5 to +5. An "0" rating was coded as a "neutral" orientation.

37. Preliminary analysis by the author of surveys conducted in 1968 and 1969 indicate, however, a slight increase in working-class support, especially among younger skilled Protestant workers. Surveys conducted by the Institut fuer angewandte Sozialwissenschaft (reported in Die Zeit, October 3, 1969: 3) found that the party in 1969 actually made gains among younger, skilled manual workers and lower-level white-collar employees, but these were not sufficient, of course, to offset the defection of so many of its traditional middle-class supporters. Also, the Institut found that almost 40% of the FDP's 1969 support consisted of 1965 nonvoters and new voters.

38. For a description of the NPD's history, program, and organization, see Kuehnl et al. (1969). A detailed analysis, employing both aggregate and survey data, of the party's vote in the state elections held between 1966 and 1968 is presented in Scheuch et al. (1969). The social-psychological bases of the party's vote and potential support are incisively analyzed in Liepelt (1967).

39. Given the very large size of these samples (for 1965, 726,000 ballots; 1969, 828,000) and the random method of their selection, these figures are very reliable.

40. Computed by the author from statistics published in the party's biannual Jahrbuch (1961, 1963, 1965, 1967, 1969).

41. See Scheuch and Klingemann (1966) for a summary of these findings. See also Almond and Verba (1963).

42. These differences, however, may be somewhat due to question text. The 1967 question was: "Generally speaking, do you consider yourself a CDU supporter, SPD supporter, FDP supporter, NPD supporter, a supporter of some other party, or don't you feel particularly attached to any party?" The question employed in 1969 called for a somewhat stronger expression of identification: "Generally speaking, do you consider youself a supporter of a particular party, or don't you feel particularly attached to any party? IF YES: Do you consider yourself a convinced supporter of −− party or not?" Neither of these questions, however is completely equivalent in formulation to the standard "party identification" question employed by the Survey Research Center: i.e., "Generally speaking, do you usually think of yourself as a Republican, a Democrat, an Independent, or what? If R or D: Would you call yourself a strong R or D, or a not very strong R or D?" Note the absence in the SRC question of an explicit "escape hatch" such as that found in the 1967 German version, i.e., "or don't you feel particularly attached to any political party." The SRC question also omits the word "supporter"; the German word "Anhaenger" connotes a stronger attachment than the English "supporter." An "Anhaenger" is probably somewhere between a habitual voter of X party and a member of that party. For the texts of the German questions, see Kaase (1970: 57-60, 82).

43. The predecessor to the BVP was the Bavarian Patriots Party (1871-1897).

44. Thirty-eight percent of the party's membership live in communities under 2,000 in population; only 13% of the membership live in cities larger than 100,000.

45. The election of Rainer Barzel at the October 1971 party conference as the new National Chairman and probable CDU/CSU Chancellor candidate in 1973 is consistent with this interpretation. Barzel's election was made possible largely by the unanimous support he received from the CSU.

46. In the Bavarian state election (November 1970), the SPD received only 33.3% of the party vote. This represents a decline of 1.3% from its 1969 performance in Bavaria (34.6%) and 2.5% drop from its poll at the 1966 state election (35.8%).

REFERENCES

ALMOND, G. and S. VERBA (1963) The Civic Culture. Princeton: Princeton Univ. Press.

BINDER, S. (1970) "Die SPD der achtziger Jahre," Die Zeit 41 (October 9, 1970): 8.

BLANKENBURG, E. (1967) Kirchliche Bindung und Wahlverhalten. Freiburg: Walter Verlag.

BLUECHER, V. G. (1962) Der Prozess der Meinungsbildung. Bielefeld: EMNID.

BURNHAM, W. D. and J. SPRAGUE (1970) "Additive and multiplicative models of the voting universe: the case of Pennsylvania, 1960-1968." Amer. Pol. Sci. Rev. 64 (June): 471-490.

BUTLER, D. and D. STOKES (1969) Political Change in Britain. New York: St. Martin's Press.

Comparative Politics (1970) 2 (July).

CONRADT, D. P. (1970) "Electoral law politics in West Germany." Pol. Studies 18 (September): 341-356.

CZEMPIEL, E. (1970) "Foreign policy issues in the West German Federal Election of 1969." Comparative Politics 2 (July): 605-628.

DAHRENDORF, R. (1967) Society and Democracy in Germany. New York: Doubleday.

Der Spiegel (1969a) 24, 21:25; 28: 26-27; 32: 26-42.

――― (1969b) 25, 6: 21-42.

――― (1969c) May 19: 30

DIEDERICH, N. (1969) "Germany," pp. 128-162 in S. Rokkan and J. Meyriat (eds.) International Guide to Electoral Statistics. Paris & The Hague: Mouton.

――― (1968) "Party member and local branch," pp. 107-115 in O. Stammer (ed.) Party Systems, Party Organizations, and the Politics of New Masses. Berlin: Institut fuer politische Wissenschaft an der Freien Universitaet Berlin.

EBERLEIN, K. (1968) Was die Deutschen Moechten. Hamburg: Wegner Verlag.

EDINGER, L. (1970) "Political change in Germany." Comparative Politics 2 (July): 549-578.

EMNID Institut (1961) Ausgewaehlte Probleme im Zusammenhang mit der Bundestagswahl 1961. Bielefeld: Mimeo.

Frankfurter Allgemeine Zeitung (1969) August 2:3; August 20:4; August 16:1; August 19:4; September 4:1.

――― (1968) November 23: 1.

HARDER, T. and F. U. PAPPI (1970) "Multiple-level regression analysis of survey and ecological data." Social Science Information 8, 5: 43-67.

HARTENSTEIN, W. and K. LIEPELT (1970) "Archives for ecological research in West Germany," pp. 555-566 in M. Dogan and S. Rokkan (eds.) Quanitative Ecological Analysis in the Social Sciences. Cambridge: MIT Press.

HIRSCH-WEBER, W. and K. SCHUETZ (1957) Waehler und Gewaehlte: Eine Untersuchung der Bundestagswahl 1953. Berlin: Wahlen Verlag.

Institut fuer angewandte Sozialwissenschaft (1969) Waehler 1969: Woher, Wohin. Bad Godesberg. (mimeo)

Institut fuer Demoskopie (1970) Waehlermeinung nicht geheim. Allensbach: Verlag fuer Demoskopie.

——— (1968) Jahrbuch der oeffentlichen Meinung, 1965-1967. Allensbach: Verlag fuer Demoskopie.

——— (1965) Jahrbuch der oeffentlichen Meinung, 1958-1964. Allensbach: Verlag fuer Demoskopie.

Jahrbuch der Sozialdemokratischen Partei Deutschlands, 1960-1961; 1962-1963; 1964-1965; 1966-1967; 1968-1969; Bad Godesberg: Neuer Vorwaerts Verlag.

KAASE, M. (1970) "Determinanten des Wahlverhaltens bei der Bundestagswahl 1969." Politische Vierteljahresschrift 11, 1: 46-110.

KAISER, C. (1971) "Triumph kroent die CDU." Die Zeit 26 (April 30): 5.

KALTEFLEITER, W. (1966) "Konsens ohne Macht, Eine Analyse der Bundestagswahl vom 19. September 1965," pp. 14-62 in F. A. Hermens (ed.) Verfassung und Verfassungswirklichkeit. Koeln and Opladen: Westdeutscher Verlag.

——— P. AREND, P. KEVENHOERSTER, and R. ZUELCH (1970) Im Wechselspiel der Koalitionen, Eine Analyse der Bundestagswahl 1969. Cologne: Carl Heymanns Verlag.

KATONA, G., B. STRUMPEL, and E. ZAHN (1971) Aspirations and Affluence, Comparative Studies in the United States and Western Europe. New York: McGraw-Hill.

KEY, V. O. (1955) "A theory of critical elections." J. of Politics 17 (February): 3-18.

KLINGEMANN, H. D. and F. U. PAPPI (1970) "Die Waehlerbewegungen bei der Bundestagswahl am 28, September 1969." Politische Vierteljahresschrift 11, 1: 111-138.

——— (1969) "Die Reaktion der Waehler auf Wahlkampf, Bundestagswahl und Regierungsbilduung 1969." Cologne. (unpublished)

——— (1968) Rechtsradikalismus in der Bundesrepublik, Cologne. (unpublished)

KUEHNL, R., R. RILLING and C. SAGER (1969) Die NPD. Struktur, Ideologie und Funktion einer neofaschistischen Partei. Frankfurt: Suhrkamp Verlag.

La PALOMBARA J. and M. WEINER (1965) "The origin and development of political parties", in J. La Palombara and M. Weiner (eds.) Political Parties and Political Development. Princeton: Princeton Univ. Press.

LEHMBRUCH, G. (1968) "The ambiguous coalition in West Germany." Government and Opposition 3 (Spring): 181-204.

LIEPELT, K. (1970) "The infra-structure of party support in Germany and Austria," pp. 183-202 in M. Dogan and R. Rose (eds.) European Politics, a Reader. Boston: Little, Brown.

——— (1968a) Electoral balance and the floating vote. Bad Godesberg: Institut fuer angewandte Sozialforschung. (unpublished)

——— (1968b) "Machtwechsel durch Mehrheitswahlrecht." Die Neue Gesellschaft 15, 5: 428-433.

――― (1967) "Anhaenger der neuen Rechtspartei." Politische Vierteljahresschrift 8, 2: 237-271.

――― and A. MITSCHERLICH (1968) Thesen zur Waehlerfluktuation. Frankfurt: Europaeische Verlagsanstalt.

LINZ, J. (1960) "The social bases of West German politics." Ph.D. dissertation. Columbia University.

LIPSET, S. M. and S. ROKKAN (1968) "Cleavage structures, party systems, and voter alignments," in S. M. Lipset and S. Rokkan (eds.) Party Systems and Voter Alignments. New York: Free Press.

MERKL, P. (1962) "Comparative study and campaign management: the Brandt campaign in Western Germany." Western Pol. Q. 15, 4: 681-704.

NOELLE-NEUMANN, E. (1969) "Was haelt der Waehler von wem?" Die Zeit 37 (September 12, 1969): 3-4.

PLOG, S. C. (1962) "The disclosure of self in the United States and Germany." J. of Social Psychology 65, 2: 193-203.

Protokoll, SPD Parteitag (1969) Bad Godesberg: Vorwaerts Verlag.

SCHEUCH, E. K. (1965) "Die Sichtbarkeit politischer Einstellungen im alltaeglichen Verhalten." Koelner Zeitschrift fuer Soziologie und Sozialpsychologie, Sonderheft No. 9: 169-214.

――― and H. D. KLINGEMANN [eds.] (1966) Rechtsradikalismus in der Bundesrepublik. Cologne: Institut fuer vergleichende Sozialforschung.

――― and T. HERZ [eds.] (1969) Die NPD in den Landtagswahlen 1966-1968. Cologne: Institut fuer vergleichende Sozialforschung.

SIMON, K. (1969) "In Bonn ist eine Stelle frei." Die Zeit 3 (January 17, 1969): 22.

SOARES, G. and R. HAMBLIN (1967) "Socio-economic variables and voting for the radical left: Chile, 1952." Amer. Pol. Sci. Rev. 61 (December): 1053-1065.

Statistisches Bundesamt [Federal Statistical Office] (1971) Wahl zum 6. Deutschen Bundestag am 28. September 1969, Reihe 8, Wiesbaden.

――― (1967) Wahl zum 5. Deutschen Bundestag am 19. September 1965, Reihe 8, Wiesbaden.

STROBEL, R. (1968) "FDP–Auf dem Weg zum Volk." Die Zeit 5 (February 2, 1968): 5.

Sueddeutsche Zeitung (1969) August 5: 2.

The Times (1969) September 25: 10.

VON BEYME, K. (1970) "The ostpolitik in the West German 1969 elections." Government and Opposition 5 (Spring): 193-217.

WEYER, W. (1970) "Machtwechsel in Bonn", pp. 19-25 in M. Nemitz (ed.) Machtwechsel in Bonn. Guetersloh: Bertelsmann Sachbuchverlag.

WILDENMANN, R. (1969) "Die Bundesrepublik am Scheideweg," in R. Wildenmann (ed.) Sozialwissenschaftliches Jahrbuch fuer Politik. Munich: Olzog Verlag.

――― (1970) "Der Zug zum Zweiparteiensystem." Publik 14 (June 26, 1970): 15.

――― and U. SCHLETH (1968) Moeglichkeiten und Grenzen der Handlungsfaehigkeit der Bundesreglerung. Mannheim University. (unpublished)

Die Zeit (1969) 24, 24: 3-5.

Zentralarchiv Data Pool (1969). Surveys conducted by the DIVO Institut for the Zentralarchiv fuer empirische Sozialforschung, Cologne University. (unpublished)

ZUNDEL, R. (1970) "Willy Brandts sanfte Rebellen", Die Zeit 10 (March 6, 1970): 8.

——— (1969a) "Die veraenderte FDP." Die Zeit 10 (March 7, 1969): 4.

——— (1969b) "Der Koalitionssegen haengt schief." Die Zeit 21 (May 23, 1969): 1.

——— (1969c) "Die sieche Koalition." Die Zeit 23 (June 6, 1969): 1.

——— (1969d) "Strategie der Parteien." Die Zeit 31 (August 1, 1969): 3.

——— (1969e) "Die Signale der Liberalen." Die Zeit 36 (September 5, 1969): 3.

DAVID P. CONRADT is Assistant Professor of Political Science at the University of Florida. His major research interests are in the areas of comparative political behavior and policy analysis. He has written several articles on West German political behavior and is the author of the forthcoming book, Public Opinion and the West German Democracy, 1949-1970.

DATE DUE